HOW DO YOU SCORE?

—Do you play dumb because you think acting smart will scare him away?

—If you don't have a date to go to a party or a bar, do you ask a platonic male friend to accompany you?

—When you ask a man to lunch, do you offer to split the bill?

—Do you find making eye contact with an attractive man exciting, or does it make you uncomfortable?

—Do you have the nerve to send a drink to that interesting-looking man sitting alone at the bar?

However you score now, you'll rate higher and do better once you've mastered the liberating strategies in—

HOW TO PICK UP A MAN

"Full of solid advice, the words, the places, the attitude and presentation."—*West Coast Review of Books*

SIGNET Books You'll Enjoy

HOW TO PICK UP A MAN

by

DIAN HANSON

With Comments by Eric Weber

A SIGNET BOOK

NEW AMERICAN LIBRARY

TIMES MIRROR

SIGNET TRADEMARK REG. U.S. PAT. OFF. AND FOREIGN COUNTRIES
REGISTERED TRADEMARK—MARCA REGISTRADA
HECHO EN CHICAGO, U.S.A.

SIGNET, SIGNET CLASSICS, MENTOR, PLUME, MERIDIAN
and NAL BOOKS are published by The New American Library,
Inc., 1633 Broadway, New York, New York 10019

First Signet Printing, May, 1983

1 2 3 4 5 6 7 8 9

PRINTED IN THE UNITED STATES OF AMERICA

For Bobby, for putting up with it all
For David, who helped
And for Randy, who typed so long and hard

Contents

HOW TO PICK UP A MAN

Comments

by Eric Weber

Ten years ago I wrote a book called *How to Pick Up Girls* that has since sold over one million copies. When it came out, many people assumed that the book was designed to show men evil, manipulative techniques for luring women into bed. But anyone who read it soon discovered that that wasn't the case at all. More than anything else, *How to Pick Up Girls* is an expression of my belief that life is vastly more fun and upbeat and romantic for those who have mastered the skill of introducing themselves to strangers than for those who quake at the prospect of talking to someone they don't know.

And that's precisely why I'm so enthusiastic about the fact that Dian Hanson has written *How to Pick Up a Man*. This lively and happy and mind-opening book shows you exactly how to introduce yourself to all those appealing men you see about you every day, on buses and planes, in supermarkets and hardware stores, on the job, at parties. And it shows you how to do it so that the man never leaps to any conclusions you don't want him leaping to . . . which seems to be the one thing women fear most about picking up a man.

Well, put your fears aside and start practicing your pick-up skills. They're going to come in very handy. We live in an increasingly fragmented society where we spend our adult years farther and farther from our roots. Young women no longer stick around in their home towns long enough to meet men through their families. They move a thousand miles away to an apartment in Chicago or Houston or Fort Lauderdale or San Francisco, which is exciting and glamorous all right but can also get kind of lonely, especially with no nice Mrs. Adamson down the block anymore to introduce you to her nephew Tom, who has come to stay with her during the holidays.

I believe that one of the antidotes to burgeoning loneliness and alienation is The Pick Up—and by that I don't mean approaching someone solely for the purpose of a one-night stand (although, if that's what you're in the mood for, I think that's just fine). No, to me picking up means nothing more than an ad hoc introduction: for example, walking up to a man in a New Wave club because you're in a mood to dance; introducing yourself to a man at a cocktail party because you overheard him mention a stock you've been following; asking a man to join you at your table in a restaurant because you loathe eating alone. You can pick up a man for an encounter as brief as a one mile jog through the park . . . or you

2

can initiate a relationship that will last a lifetime. The chapters that follow teach you how to do it all, gracefully and creatively. And if you're worried about being a pioneer, don't be. Ten years ago there were very few women who picked up men; in fact, it was mostly the other way around. But about three to four years back the tide began turning . . . so radically, in fact, that now it's commonplace for women to walk up to men and introduce themselves. And if you find that hard to believe, just watch carefully at the next party or art gallery opening you attend. I suspect you'll find as many women approaching men as vice versa. Which is great, when you think about it. For the more normal it becomes, the less nervous and different you will feel about doing it and the less likely a man is to misinterpret your intentions.

So read on. Suddenly, you'll realize that there are a lot more appealing men well within your orbit than you ever dreamed possible. And when that happens, it's just a matter of time before you pluck one (or many) out of the crowd for your very own.

1

Once Upon a Time . . .

In 1979 I was twenty-eight years old and going somewhere. I finally had a job I liked, to my amazement there were clothes in my closet, and my six foot frame had finally achieved fashionable grace. After years of gawky shyness I was finally becoming comfortable with myself. I learned I could dance real dances, I could converse, I could charge things and I could even order in a French restaurant without getting hives.

It was a very good life but surprisingly sometimes lonely. I never minded being alone, as I'd been alone so much as a child, but every once in a while I minded having no one to share with. I knew men and how to meet men, but being so busy I slipped into seeing men who were nice men, good men, but not the fantasies I once pursued. Until I picked up that man in November.

I was working and so was he. It was my job to see that two models, scheduled for photo sessions the next day, enjoyed their tour of New York nightclubs. His job was to photograph their enjoyment. I watched his bright eyes and his soft brown hair and listened to his clever wit, and it occurred to me that I liked him. It also occurred to me that if I let the evening take its natural course, he would leave and I would end up baby-sitting the two girls, as usual.

I looked him in the eye, took a deep breath and decided, "I think the girls have worked enough for tonight. Why don't you come and dance?" He grinned and agreed and followed me onto the floor.

The girls tucked themselves in bed and I rediscovered the fun of fantasies.

Two years later I was lying in bed with that man I picked up in November.

"What did you like about me that first night?" I wheedled.

"The fact that you knew all the real dances," he teased.

"Why did you decide to spend the evening with me instead of the two models?" I pushed.

"For the same reason I married you," he murmured, nudging me over and snuggling into my back. "You gave me no choice."

"What do you mean?"

"You picked me up. What could I do?"

"I never picked you up."

"You did and I loved you for it. You should be proud. Of your good taste."

"It's funny. It made me feel defensive when you said that. When I was fourteen a nasty rumor went around the school. Two boys were spreading the word that over summer vacation I'd met them at an amusement park and tried to pick them both up. You know, I was really unpopular; they said they *knew* I was desperate but had never figured it was *that* bad. It never happened, but I wanted to quit school just to escape them and all the horrible comments. Things didn't cool down till after Christmas."

"Poor baby."

"It's amazing that words have so much power."

"Um huh."

"And what ruined my life then, made you love me."

"Umm."

"You know, most women I know still feel funny about picking up men."

"That's why they call you and moan about not meeting any men. The guys are ready. Didn't I fall in love with you?"

"Yeah. Maybe you're different."

"No I'm not. Let's turn out the light."

"Why do you think they don't know the men feel like that?"

"I dunno. Why don't you write a book? In the morning."

* * *

What *does* pick up mean? When I was fourteen it meant tainted and dirty. It set a woman apart and said that she was "fast" or not "nice."

So how did we jump to the present when a woman can pick up a man and have him fall in love with her? We did it by jumping over the lie of sexless womanhood.

In ten years we've made fantastic strides. We've discovered our bodies and how to unlock their pleasure centers. We can take pride in the curves that attract men and joy in arousing those men. We're also coming to openly enjoy male bodies and learning which kinds of men hold special appeal for us. We know who we are and who we'd like to spend our time with and suddenly we reach an unbridgeable gap. How do we connect with the man we want as friend and lover? The bridge is that old dirty phrase, pick up.

"Why do women talk so big and act so small? With all their talk about being equal with men, I started to think they meant it. As long as I'm eating well I don't mind if they have a good job, and I don't mind washing dishes or changing a dirty diaper, if it came up, but what I do mind is doing all this and then still having to beg for a date, pay all the bills and read her mind as to whether she wants to make love when we get back to her five-hundred-dollar-a-month apartment. If women would be equal in love, we'd give them the world!" So speaks a confused and frustrated man, twenty-seven years old and working his way up on Wall Street. He's a man you might want to meet, and he wishes, as the majority of men do today, that you would meet him halfway.

"But why should I pick him up?" asks my friend Annette. "If we meet *some* way, why does it matter who makes the first move?" For one thing, if he does not come on to you, there may be no other way you will meet. But much more important is that the way you begin your relationship sets the tone for all that follows. Many women still want to be swept into romance, carried away by a passionate and commanding man. Then, as the relationship sours, this kind of woman complains that he is what? Too commanding. She sees serious relationships as an interruption, a time-out from her life. While these women are involved with a man, they take on his interests, his friends, even his eating and dressing habits. Eventually a woman like this is no longer the same woman he met and carried off. His interest wanders, and she's left feeling angry and cheated.

On the other hand, when you approach a man first, he knows you have a strong sense of yourself. If he responds, he shows that he likes that strength and there's a good chance he will encourage you to stay an individual and not try to turn you into an accessory in his life. When you learn to communicate your own life goals, you will be able to achieve them and form better relationships.

And lest you still worry that men are not ready for you to pick them up, you have closed your eyes to the liberating strides they have taken over the last ten years. Most are happy with our freer lives and have come quietly to agree with women in their views on love, sex and romance. I've seen them looking across the gap that keeps us from approaching a man who intrigues us and wishing that we would bridge it, so that they could cross it themselves.

Cross the bridge. Those junior high gossips are long gone. When you see that man you'd like to spend your time with, you have no reason to hesitate. The eighties is the age of sharing, but you must reach out to get your piece of this great new world.

2

Exploding the Myths

It's so easy to believe in the theory of picking up
men. So easy, because theory is miles away from
action. When you are faced with a real man, a man
alone and quite accessible, theory tends to give
way to myth and irrational fear. You can't approach
him. Why? Fearful Myth #1, you say.

*The only women who pick up men are women
whom no man would want. He'll assume something's wrong with me.*

Is there? Is something seriously wrong with you,
something that has kept you from ever having a
date? Do children point at you on the street and
polite citizens turn away? There are so very few of
us who could answer yes that I'll assume a no. All
a man sees is what you project. If you're relaxed,
smiling and friendly, he'll just assume you're a
smiling, friendly woman. Unless there's something
wrong with him.

Ah, but what I really meant was Myth #2:

Most men are intimidated by a woman taking the initiative and usurping their masculine role.

You *can* intimidate men. The most effective ways are dressing so sexy that you arouse him and then treating his arousal with disdain; smiling and meeting his gaze, only to treat him coldly when he speaks to you; and staring at his groin and smirking. It's confusing communication that makes men most uncomfortable. As my friend Richard says, "Is she staring at me because she likes me, or have I stained my shirt?" When you show a genuine, spoken interest in a man you *reinforce* his masculinity by telling him he's desirable.

Is that reinforcement what I really want? I worry about Myth #3.

He'll assume I want to go straight to bed, no matter what I say or do, because a woman that forward is probably an easy lay.

Men hope to go to bed with all women they find attractive. His wanting it is a compliment, appreciation you can enjoy without needing to reward. And if you're honest, instant desire it not alien to you. Part of your wanting to meet him is wanting to make love. *Time* is the difference. Maybe you want to get to know him well enough before going to bed. If you worry that a man will think you "fast" or "easy," don't project that image. The simple act of approach does not label you fast. An attractive woman starting an unexpected conversation is better described as intriguing, and the more intriguing he finds you, the more control you have over when you bed.

I've read the papers. I've seen the movies. What about #4?

Picking up a man may trigger the prudish psychotic impulses of "Goodbar" types. How do I know I won't get a rapist or worse?

Truly twisted individuals are very rare, and those who believe it is their duty to punish tramps are usually aggressively stalking them in the places they consider the most contaminated. That leads them to singles bars, hotels frequented by hookers, strip clubs, topless bars—the places, in short, where sinners will be most abundantly available. The only one of these places you are likely to go unescorted is the singles bar, and as I will point out in later chapters, this is not the best place to meet men anyway. One reason the best approaches to men are nonflirty is that they help you avoid the sickies. If a man uses violent expressions ("I'd like to strangle that meter maid!") when the situation doesn't really warrant them, say, "Nice to meet you, goodbye," *while still in a public spot.*

Good enough, but not all fears are of injury. I could be mentally dragged down, like by Myth #5:

Only "wimps" are turned on by women aggressive enough to take the advantage.

Yes, submissive Milquetoasts will throw themselves in your path if there's a chance you'll be their mama. But think first that aggressive is not the same as assertive. An aggressive approach hints at violence, at an angry push behind your step forward. Assertive just means making your interests known, and assertive women aren't as likely to activate a submissive or masochistic man. Example: the aggressive woman commands, "You're just what I've been looking for. Let's have a drink." The assertive woman quietly says: "Hi, having another drink? Mind if I have one with you?" An assertive woman leaves room for options. He's free to say no and he *must* take the stand of saying yes to keep things rolling. If these decisions are too hard for him, perhaps you've found a man too wimpy to interest you. Have your drink and depart. Who says you can't step over the man who throws himself in your path and move on to a stronger one?

You're right, that sounds easy, but here's a sticky one. I count on men taking me out. How do I avoid Myth #6?

If I pick up a man he may expect me to pay for drinks, dinner, etc.

He probably won't, but I recommend splitting the bill anyway. Why erase this little pleasure of free meals? Because life is getting expensive, as you've already noted, and paying for a date is now a considerable investment. If the man you select is money-conscious, his budget may eliminate your favorite restaurants, theaters or clubs from the agenda, and whether he is or isn't financially squeezed, he's more

likely to consider the return on moneys laid out.
You'll feel stronger maintaining control by paying
your share of the evening, because when you go
Dutch you're obligated to nothing. If you have
fun, you share the fun. If it's less than you hoped,
there are no hard feelings or wrestling scenes in the
hall.

That one I'll have to think about. I really don't
want to feel used, which also brings to mind Myth
#7.

*If a man picks me I know he's really attracted to
me. If I pick him, how do I know he's really as
interested?*

Think again. A man may pick you up for any
number of reasons having nothing to do with love at
first sight. Maybe you were the only woman smiling
at him, or perhaps you look like his sister and concentrating on that made it possible for him to approach you. It may even be something as stereo-
typed as his believing that women with big breasts
are oversexed and he wouldn't feel guilty about spending one night with you, if it goes that way. When a
man approaches you, he may be infatuated—and tell
you that. More likely he means you're cute and he'd
like to know if your personality matches up. When
you approach him, you flatter him with your good
taste, triggering him to think you're pretty cute *and*
have a great personality.

But, but, but. If this is all so much fun, consider
Myth #8:

I could get hooked on shallow encounters and "scoring."

Very few people like a different date every night. For the most part this is something that sounds good around the water cooler and makes for a very lonely reality. If you keep every new man an acquaintance, what does it say for your self-image? It says you're scared. Plain scared to let anyone get close enough to discover your frailties, your humanness. If you haven't courted this kind of isolation in the past, it won't develop now no matter how much you enjoy taking the initiative. Picking up men won't erode a normally warm nature.

I give up. There is one last one you can't refute, though; #9 never changes:

My mother will die.

If mothers weren't the strongest creatures conceivable, would they be given the responsibility of rearing such thankless daughters? Seriously, if you're over eighteen, you're old enough for a private life. If your mother is truly fragile, look up the definition of private and apply it more diligently.

Let's hope that we have now disposed of the mythology. There are so many men right now hoping a woman like yourself will help them to know you that it makes no sense to wait. Except to wait for the right one. Men really do cherish a woman bold enough to take the first step, but you know that not all men you approach will respond. It may be that you are not right for him, just as you may find in talking to him that he is not right for you. When you adopt the assertiveness formerly reserved for men, you enter their world of hits and misses. Only a few people will really fit with you in a magical way, blending visual appeal and interests with that electrochemical spark. You'll realize you really don't want to pick up every man you approach. If the charge doesn't flow for him as well as you, be grateful he lets you know. You aren't racking up scores in some game where no win means you lose. Picking up men is more like a casting call for deeper relationships. There are many, many who will read for the part before that magic clicks. Meeting, testing, trying out, are vital exercises for finding true friends and lasting relationships. Every audition should be a new adventure and every bad reading a step toward the next and better one.

3

Ten Men Tell You
How They Feel

That last chapter was a fine high-minded sermon, you're saying. But will the man I pick up really respond in the spirit in which I approach him? Why are you so sure men are really ready to abandon the double standard?

The reason I'm so sure is that I've done a lot of research. In addition to interviewing hundreds of men in the course of my work as an editor for *Oui*, I handed ten attractive men the following questionnaire:

A. Would you let a woman pick you up?

B. Have you ever been picked up by a woman and if so, how?

C. What is the approach you would like best?

D. Does getting picked up undermine your masculine role?

E. Do you assume that it's always going to have to be you who makes the first move?

F. Do you consider a woman cheap for introduc-

ing herself to you? If so, what can she do to dissuade you from thinking that she is "that kind of girl"?

Here are their answers:

A. Would you let a woman pick you up?

Ten positive answers, ranging from a simple yes to a gladly, a definitely, all the way up to a few manic Absolutelys!

B. Have you ever been picked up by a woman and if so, how?

Seven yeses, three nos. What follows are the more interesting examples:

Robert: I was sitting across the aisle from a woman on the Metroliner from Washington to New York. The train started with a tremendous lurch and I looked around in amazement, wanting to share my fear with some of the other passengers. The woman sitting across the aisle from me smiled and said, "Incredible, huh?" "Yeah," I said, "and I took the train because I'm not exactly crazy about flying."

We started talking, and she moved over to the seat next to me before I even thought of getting near her. She was getting off in Philadelphia, so she suggested we make a date to see each other over the weekend. On my way back from New York I stopped off in Philly and we spent two terrific days together. We're still going out, all because she said, "Incredible, huh?" If she hadn't, I doubt that I would have spoken to her. I've never felt comfortable talking to a stranger unless he or she speaks to me first.

Alex: I was playing chess in a bar with a friend. The waitress came over and watched for a while, said she always admired men with the intellect to play chess. My friend and I laughed because we were both unbelievably bad at the game. Then a short time later, she came back and said to me that she was about to take her break and would I like to come around the corner and have a cup of coffee with her. I winked at my friend and said, "See you in about a week, Mike." As soon as we sat down, the waitress smiled at me and said the reason she was drawn to me was that I looked very much like a professor of hers. I sat back in my chair, regarding her smugly, just waiting for her to pop the question, "Why don't we go up to my apartment?" Something about my attitude must have annoyed her because about ten seconds later she said, "You know, just because I asked you to have a cup of coffee doesn't mean we're going to go to bed. You just looked nice, like somebody I'd like to get to know." I felt like an idiot. We returned to the bar, me to my chess game, she to her job. Later, she and my friend and I went out to a party together. She was friendly, but not very. At the party, she met an old boyfriend and they left together. I was depressed at not having been more sensitive to her feelings. She had to find out if there was something about me that she could respond to *beyond* her initial attraction. That happened over ten years ago. Ever since, I've never felt that just because a woman spoke to me first that that was tantamount to us hopping into bed. I always assume that she is attracted on a superficial level by my appearance and that now it is up to both of us to see if we like each other's personalities.

Hal: I was in college at the time. It was between classes, and I was sitting having a Coke at a dingy campus hangout. At the table next to me I recognized a girl from my political science class. We had never spoken, and I had no idea of whether she recognized me since it was a huge lecture class with over two hundred students. Anyway, I found her very pretty. She had long blond hair and full sensuous lips, and I began to think that if I had any balls I would get up and introduce myself. But the closer I came to actually doing it, the more nervous I became. Then all of a sudden she got up, picked up her cup of coffee, and walked over to me. "Do you mind if I sit and talk with you until class begins?" she said. Mind? I was ecstatic. My social life was the absolute pits at the time. The only thing that bothered me a little was that she had displayed more courage than I. She sat down, we talked, walked to class together, and *I* got up the courage to ask her out. She accepted. We dated all through college and it was one of the greatest relationships of my life.

Ted: A go-go girl in a discothèque was being bothered by a customer, so she told him that I was her boyfriend. Later she apologized for putting me on the spot and asked me to drive her home. When we got there she said she couldn't ask me in for a drink but she'd like to see me again. I called her for a date later that week.

Douglas: This took place in a bar. I walked in; she and I looked at each other; she said "You look like you could use a drink"; we talked, and within fifteen minutes she made it quite clear that I had no choice. I was hers for the evening. We're still going out. I guess in a way I kind of like being dominated by a woman. My mother was a very commanding person.

Carl: She joined a small group of us who were standing around talking at a party, and while she was standing next to me she put her hand in mine and playfully caressed it, vamping, sort of. That took the curse off it. She was playing the part of the seductress, but not really being one. I laughed. I thought it was terribly funny. Plus it tickled. We went to bed that night. It was unbelievably sensational.

Gil: It was at a company picnic. I was sitting in the grass watching a softball game, feeling a little funny because I was by myself and most everyone else seemed to be married or with someone. A woman walked up and said, "Hi, I'm Emily." That's it, nothing more. But it sure was enough for me. We started talking. Four months later we were married. Today we have three kids, just because she had the boldness to walk up and say, "Hi." Unbelievable!

C. What is the approach you would like best?
Here the overwhelming consensus was that a woman's first words should be direct, complimenting them, making them laugh, showing an interest in them. For example:

Alex: Something trivial . . . like "Great band, isn't it?" or "You look bored," as long as she seems friendly.

Michael: Just be nice, ask me about what I'm doing.

Robert: Direct . . . whatever is natural. I like it when a woman asks my advice.

Carl: Take an interest in the newspaper or magazine I'm reading, like on a bus on the way to work.

Gil: All a girl has to say is hello and Boom! A guy responds immediately. If she backs that up with something really interesting or a joke maybe, it's really fantastic.

Joseph: I think guys are less aware of women using lines than vice versa, so I think she could say anything. It's easy for a woman to pick up a guy, because it's every man's fantasy. He'd seize upon her every word. Just be nice, so he doesn't think you're a tramp.

D. Does getting picked up undermine your masculine role?

Here the answer was universal—No. Not one man said he was offended or felt emasculated by a woman's making the first move. I was very happy to hear this and pass it on to my friends who use it as their #1 rationale *not* to approach a man. "He won't like me," they claim, "because he's going to feel I'm usurping his role." I have always felt that men were eager to share some of these roles, that what those women were saying was that they were afraid to take action . . . and apparently the men I interviewed agree. As one man, a lawyer in his mid-thirties, put it:

No . . . no . . . it's more important for the woman to make the first move, for ultimately it's really she who determines whether or not you're going to have a relationship. Why shouldn't she choose the man she really wants in the first place, rather than go through the charade that it's really the man's choice, which is an illusion that wastes a lot of people's time. Instead of her waiting around for eight guys to approach so she can pick out the one she's really had her eye on all along, why doesn't she just go up to the one she wants and save the other seven guys the time and embarrassment?

E. Do you assume that it's always going to have to be you who makes the first move?

Here again the men were in universal agreement. Their feeling is that if they don't talk to a woman first, ask her to dance, phone her for a date, then they simply are not going to meet anyone. Most of them were thrilled by the prospect of women doing some of the initiating. For example:

Ted: I do assume it's my responsibility to initiate an introduction. Although I don't like it . . . that's reality. If you don't approach a woman you're attracted to, 99 percent of the time you won't meet her. I don't think it undermines my masculine role when it happens . . . it's flattering, very good for the ego.

Douglas: I love the idea of us sharing the responsibility. It's such a strain always to have to be the one who's risking rejection.

Carl: It would be nice for a change. It would take some of the load off a man's shoulders.

F. Do you consider a woman cheap for introducing herself to you?

Here is another excuse that many women use to avoid the responsibility of taking their social lives into their own hands. "Men will think of me as a one night stand." Is this true? Well, it is and it isn't. From my interviews I found that less educated and inexperienced men are more apt to believe that a woman who talks to them first is looking for sex. Men who have been to college, professional men, artists, men over twenty-five, and those who have already been married don't even address the issue. First they know instant gratification doesn't come that easy. Second, they're more likely to admire a woman who will exercise her sexual rights immediately and they will want a second date all the more if she shows her erotic side on the first date. This also bore out what I have long believed—most men do not look down on women who express normal sexual impulses. As more and more women admit to sex lives, they also discover that men love them for their healthy sexual responses. It's especially gratifying to discover that the more thoughtful and intelligent men are the freest in this respect. To wit,

Alex: I much prefer women who are sexually open to those who feel it is ennobling to wait several weeks or months before going to bed with me. I mean, why kid around? It seems so childish and petty. The women I have fallen in love with have almost in-

26

variably been those women I've slept with the first night I've met them. I find them more exciting and fun, more full of life and guts and danger.

Louis: What is this easy and not easy? A woman is a human animal, just like a man. Some people turn you on and you want to go make love to them right away. And some people you have to get to know better before you start feeling drawn to them sexually. I know I work that way, and I'm sure a lot of women do, too. If a woman sleeps with me the first night, I don't think she's cheap. I think she finds something about me so attractive, so special, she just doesn't want to wait. If she doesn't want to sleep with me, I figure we have to get to know each other a little better.

When you don't feel a powerful attraction to a new man, it's nice to see that *most* men do not assume a woman is theirs for the night because she has made the first move.

Hal: If a woman comes up to me, I don't assume anything except that she probably likes my appearance . . . and there ain't nothing wrong with that.

Louis: When I was younger I thought that every woman who approached me was a victim of love at first sight. Bitter experience has disabused me of that notion. I can't tell you how many times nothing more came of it than a few minutes of conversation and then the woman went on to talk to somebody else. What I really think is happening when a woman introduces herself to a man is that she's looking to see if there's anything more there than an initial attraction. If there is, fantastic. If there isn't, no harm done.

Robert: I've had women ask me to dance and it's turned out that they only wanted someone to dance with, not to take them home. You can't assume anything with the women of today. They're self-interested and assertive, just like we [men] are. It's scary, but it's also more exciting.

CONCLUSION

What are these men really saying? What my whole book is telling you. Do it, talk to them. You won't be the first. Whether they say it or not, many women are already approaching men, and the good men go fast. It's just one more area in which women —justifiably—are coming into their own, and the men you want are happy about it.

4

Psyching Up

If you're an outgoing woman, you may not believe that leaving the house can be the hardest step in meeting men. Shy women know. Shyness makes one fear the scrutiny of others and many women, including myself in years not so far past, can anticipate a party with pleasure only until the moment comes to walk out the door. Suddenly your clothes feel wrong, tension tightens your chest, your head may ache, all conspiring to make an excuse for not going out. Staying home is not very hard for a shy woman. Not meeting any men is the killer.

Home psyching is a simple set of rituals that will help any woman setting out to pick up a man. For the shy woman it has real significance. Preparing your mood before you reach the door can make the difference between walking through it and another night of Mork and Mindy. Choose the tips that increase your confidence, or use them as a guide for developing your own. No woman should be a prisoner in her own home when the world is so full of men.

Put on the perfume that makes you feel bold and capricious. Look for the evening blends, the muskier, earthy ones rather than light scents. Applied in the hollow of your throat, your perfume will reach you every time you speak or turn your head, making you feel attractive and rich in appeal.

Wear your most beautiful lingerie—not because a man may take your clothes off, or because you might be run over by a bus and be undressed in some emergency room, but so you can cherish the secret of extravagant beauty hiding beneath your shy exterior. A secret is probably what put the famous smile on the Mona Lisa, and a wonderful secret can make you feel special in a room full of strangers.

Wear a piece of jewelry with personal significance. A smooth ring can be discreetly stroked when you're nervous to calm you like worry beads. It may even be a ring given to you by an old love, not a man you still pine for, but one who made you happy and whose expression of love, represented in a ring or necklace, will remind you that men can enjoy your company.

Change yourself. A new lipstick color, a haircut or trim, or curling your hair if you always wear it straight is a big morale booster for many women. You feel new, beautiful, reborn and you really do become prettier all over when you feel good.

One warning: don't get too dependent on change

to lift your spirits. One aspiring model I know became friends with a plastic surgeon. She'd always been very insecure about her looks, which were not really bad, and when she met a doctor who'd treat her for free, she became addicted to "corrective" surgery. Every time an important new job opportunity came up, she rushed in for a little snipping and plasticizing to correct the flaws she felt would jeopardize her getting the work. By the end of two years she'd undergone three breast operations, three nose alterations, two chin implants, cheek implants and a buttock tuck. She became so artificial that she was turned down for jobs because of it. And there's no going back at that point. A little change is a lift, too much is self-destruction.

While you're getting ready to go out, put on a record that makes you feel lively and energized. I used to rely on hard rock to psych me for evenings out, and if I was really feeling shaky there was nothing like Janis Joplin's "Turtle Blues" from her *Cheap Thrills* album. It's a bluesy, ballsy anthem to taking charge of your love life.

Dance, exercise and get your body moving. Try undulating to that record you put on. You'll never dissipate the nervous energy you're storing up while you sit still, so use it up in physical activity. Don't push for exhaustion. Just move around enough to feel pleasantly warmed up and limber, ready to take on the world.

Read a chapter from a beautifully written book, a

classic novel perhaps. Besides the distraction of reading, immersing yourself in stimulating language makes your conversation more creative. If you write, that's even better. Put down some lines on a subject you're impassioned about, then take that exhilaration out into the evening.

Put on the right shoes; they affect our moods more than any other clothing. When you wear teetery stiletto heels you look sexy but are limited in your movements and forced into a more passive mode. Tennis shoes make you bouncy and brash, one of the boys. Boots set a dominant tone. Think how you feel when you wear different kinds of shoes and choose the pair that will give you the most freedom and positive image of yourself.

Lastly, fix in your mind that you're going out to have fun, the best time possible. You're not obligated to please any man. You're going out to make yourself happy and whether you return home with a new friend or alone is unimportant compared to getting through the door and enjoying it.

FORETHOUGHT

Sometimes you will see a man you want to meet when you had no expectations of meeting anyone. You must make a move quickly or the moment will be past; he'll be gone and you'll be kicking yourself. Here are some quick mental and physical exercises to calm you for the big step up to him. Use what works for you.

Relax your breathing. Touch your fingertips to your diaphragm, located about four or five inches above your navel, and breathe slowly and deeply so that you feel your diaphragm expand. Think of the tension flowing out with the breath. Three good slow breaths will make you feel much calmer.

Bend your knees a little. Shake your shoulders and arms loose. Roll your head from side to side and generally shake the tension from your muscles. Concentrate on the stiffness running off the tips of your fingers and out through your toes.

Relax your stomach. We tend to clench our abdominal muscles when we're anxious. Let your stomach push out against your clothes so you can feel the expansion. Better to show him a bit of bulge than stand transfixed with fear.

Correct your posture. Many of us hunch over when we're feeling vulnerable, like a rabbit making himself small and invisible to the hawk. You won't be hurt by speaking to a man. If you throw back your shoulders you'll present a more confident, appealing image, and your limbs will hang less stiffly.

Call an image into your mind that makes you feel strong. When you find one that works, you can use it all the time and bring it up instantly. Practice now before you see him. Maybe it's remembering that time you got your name in the paper that makes you feel powerful, or the time you made a difficult decision, stood by it and were proved right. It could be the memory of another time you got up the nerve to approach a man you had a great time with, or a man who picked you up who was nervous himself and whom you helped to calm. Hold your thought as you approach this new man, keeping it until you get caught up enough to really enjoy yourself.

Fantasize him holding you, caressing you in the way you love most. There's a tremendous energy in sexual thoughts, they motivate and make us bold. You don't have to express any of these thoughts to him, just yet, but let them buoy you along.

Bribe yourself. "If I walk up and start a conversation with that good-looking man, I'll get to go buy those tortoiseshell hair combs I've been wanting." Tie the two pleasures together and courage comes easier.

Remind yourself that men have gone to extraordinary lengths all through history to pick up women. They have a primal love of women, an attraction much deeper than needing a date for Saturday night. When you speak to a man, you are giving him the green light to express the interest that is always there, active or dormant. He is more naturally predisposed to like you than reject you, so don't run off after the first sentence. Give his feelings a chance to reveal themselves.

34

Smile and keep smiling. If he's initially cool, it's most likely because you have surprised him. Many people react to unexpected situations with ugly behavior. Aloofness or aggressive comments may be his way of testing your interest. "Is she serious? Let me be a pig for a minute and find out if she'll put up with it." If you keep your humor and your own good spirits he'll quickly join in. Never forget that he has his own insecurities to deal with.

And you have yours. Many shy women also appear aloof and disdainful in an attempt to hide their inner quaking. If he walks away, well, it was because you didn't really want to know him in the first place. Don't fool yourself and miss the fun for fear of losing. You're *gaining* when you take control of your social life.

When you've found the exercises that work for you in psyching for pick up, and when you've banished aloofness, there's only one hint left for preparing for a happier, fuller social life. That is *projecting affection*. I've already mentioned smiling. Think, too, of looking a man in the eyes and thinking of what you like about him as you talk. Think of his soulful brown eyes, the way the corners of his mouth lift when he talks, the way he uses his hands. Concentrate on the pleasure those things give you, and he will see the affection in your eyes. There is nothing that makes a person more attractive. You can prove it to yourself. Look at a photograph of yourself taken by a stranger. Compare it to one taken by a person you loved. Looking into the lens of someone you love, you become prettier in every line and feature. That's why I, who hate having my picture taken, like the photographs my husband, Bobby, does of me. Warmth is beauty. You can see it in photographs, and the man who's looking into your happy eyes will see it and want to see more of you.

Dian Hanson

5

Girl Friends, Gay Friends and Other Women's Men

I have a cousin who was a knockout at sixteen. We went to the same school, the school where my nickname was "That Weirdo" and she was a queen. She was willowy, blond and tall, this cousin, and she allowed me to be her friend that year. As her friend I went on dates with her because she wasn't allowed out alone, and it seemed that every handsome, popular boy had a friend with a car, something the popular boy never had. My cousin had the popular boy and the backseat. I had the front seat and the friend with the car, given him to atone for acne, buck teeth, jug ears and other sundry curses. By no stretch of imagination were these double dates. My cousin and her boy in the back were on a date, kissing and giggling and having a great time, while the poor boy with the car drove and I stared out the window and learned to deeply resent my cousin.

At twenty-three I had a friend who loved to dance. We went to singles bars together, where I enjoyed my first taste of popularity and she was—

my friend with the car. I called her my *best* friend at twenty-three, but I left her standing at the bar all the time and ran off to have long conversations with men who had no friend for her, or none interested in her, and sometimes I kissed and giggled with men in the backseat of her car while she drove us home and stared out the window. And though she was my best friend she learned to deeply resent me.

Both my cousin and my friend were women whom I enjoyed and valued. Each helped me through a difficult time in life—my cousin helped me to win acceptance in high school, and my girl friend taught me to dance and recover from a difficult relationship. We were close without jealousies, conflicts or cattiness, and so it was natural that we mixed our friendships with our romances. Natural, and disastrous to those friendships. When most of us think of going to a bar, restaurant or party, we think of taking a friend along for company. When you just want to drink, eat or dance it's great. When you're fantasizing about meeting a man, go out alone.

First of all, if you're over twenty, going out with your girl friends can make you look like a gang of losers, unfair for all of you, but it's the same feeling *you* have when you see single men walk into a party together. The consensus? They couldn't get dates.

So here you are at the party with your friends, and while you're all sizing up the situation, how do you make yourselves comfortable? Often by cutting up the people around you to amuse each other. Fun when you're nervous, but if you're overheard, it reinforces the view that you're losers, and even if no one hears, it sets a mood among you that's hard to break when you do start mingling. The minute you or one of your friends start concentrating on a man, the Great Hatchet Job goes into action. Have you ever played this game? You talk to a man for twenty minutes. He excuses himself to go to the bathroom and you ask your friends, "What do you think?" And they all start in: "Did you see those shoes? Where'd he buy them, off a retired beat cop?" "Did you notice how his Adam's apple jumps when he swallows?" "The way he waves his hands around, he reminds me of that used car salesman on Channel 39." They're just having fun, carrying on in the same vein as you did at the beginning of the party, but now you're more sensitive, and while you laugh, you listen, and when he comes back out he doesn't look quite the same. You are more sensitive to all criticism when you're meeting a man because you're extending yourself, becoming vulnerable to judgment by making a choice for the world to see, and when your friends offer even joking jabs you're likely to listen and try to please them more than yourself. It's not fair to you and certainly not fair to the man.

Sometimes your friends will criticize a man you've approached with no joke intended. This is even harder to handle. If you respect your friend's opinions it's very hard to tell if her objections just reflect her different tastes in men or real insight into a fatal flaw. Do you listen to her or to him or to yourself? You can be the only judge, but if she really objects to him and she has the car, you may be forced to choose her company over his. Again, not fair.

And what if you get engrossed with your new friend and your girl friend has found no one to talk to? You can include her as much as possible but it still comes down to the question of where you put your loyalties. If she feels sullen and neglected none of you has a good time.

Competition. It's not supposed to exist between friends, but there are always exceptions and your friend may feel that the man you like is the man she has to have. She doesn't want to hurt you any more than you do her, so it all starts out friendly. But if he fails to show a preference or makes one that seems easily shaken, this is when your trusted friend will let slip that you once considered having a former boyfriend's initials tattooed on your posterior. Or when you will mention what a wonderful plastic surgeon she has, er, knows.

Some men will enjoy seeing two women compete for their attention, but most are frightened away. The woman who plays too mean worries him as much as she does you. A good way to fight competition when it does arise, then, is to pretend it's not happening. Be nice to her, be nice to him, and let the man draw the comparisons.

The last thing to consider in deciding whether to

go out with your girl friend is, what if all these situations were reversed? She meets the fascinating man and you sit and wait and watch and wish like hell there was a window to stare out.

GAY FRIENDS

I'm speaking of gay male friends, the kind many of us have and love and save all our best secrets for. To a heterosexual woman, a gay man is a wonderful blend of girl friend and boyfriend. We can share thoughts and experiences with a gay man we'd never dare tell to a girl friend for fear she'd think them too—unmentionable. He will listen to a daring sexual fantasy with relish and without telling us we're sick, as a girl friend may, or thinking we're asking to have it played out, as a heterosexual man may. A gay friend can more wholly enjoy man-watching with us than many woman friends, because he understands this harmless voyeuristic impulse for what it is. Finally, I've found that gay friends really enjoy getting dressed in formal clothing and taking you for a snobby, elegant night on the town more than any hetero man I've ever known.

Now, the danger with gay men.

The primary danger is that you may forget that your friend is first and foremost a man. He's not a girl friend in briefs, and when you arrange to spend an evening out with him, it's very possible to offend him by approaching other men. Not, as many believe, because he is competing with you for their attention, but because he was raised like any other man, and when he's out with a date, he wants to be shown the respect that you would show anyone else. Unless you've prearranged to split up and seek others, you should stay with him and enjoy his company.

A gay man can, however, be the platonic friend you take to a bar or party, as described in The Basics of Approach. If you've agreed you're both going out with the intent of meeting new people, then you *may* find him indulging in a little competition. It's a simpler problem than with girl friends, generally. Most men will have strong sexual preferences and will let you know right away if they're more interested in you or in him.

Your gay friends are a fun addition to your life, but like girl friends, if you depend on their company every time you go out, you'll limit your opportunities to meet other men.

OTHER WOMEN'S MEN

Lately I've discovered a new kind of assertive woman. She's the legendary predatory female, a woman who will actually walk up to a man when he's clearly with another woman and try to pick him up.

When I first began researching this book, Ann R., a chic woman in her early fifties, said to me, "How

do you get a man if he's already with a woman?"
I was flabbergasted. "What I want to know," she
continued, "is how do you get him to leave her and
go with you? And what about married men?"

It's not my intention to tell women how to seduce
married men. Some may argue that's because I'm
married myself and sensitive to women taking my
husband, but I don't think so. Going after a man
who's with another woman is hostile to the man
and to the woman. If you can get him away, what
do you have? A disloyal man, who can leave you
in the same way, thereby proving to you what you
perhaps believed when you went after him—that no
man is trustworthy. You can get a certain pleasure
from educating his present companion in the same
bitter lesson, but why? To put her in your position,
thus rendering her more equal to yourself? We
could all use less envy.

There are so many men in the world, approxi-
mately two billion, that there really is no man you
have to have. If you like him and he's not available,
ask him if he has any friends. That's flattering, and
he may have a single friend who shares his interests, profession and level of good looks. Most of us
choose friends very similar to ourselves.

Retain him as a friend. Many times you'll find
yourself drawn to a man because he's a nice person
to talk to and you share many interests. All those
things will still be yours as a friend, and if that
woman he's with is a girl friend rather than a wife,

they may part ways in the future. Just don't hang around waiting for it to happen. If you can't selflessly enjoy his and her friendship without pushing for more, move on to unfenced pasture.

It's wonderful to enjoy new freedoms, but remember that not quite *all* the world is your oyster. When you tread on the freedom of others, they're less likely to respect yours.

6

The Active/Passive Quiz

As we all are of different heights, weights and intelligence, so are we different energy types. Some of us leap out of bed with the sun, eager for the day and the chance to stretch our minds and bodies, believing that sleep is an annoying necessity, an unwelcome break in our pursuit of goals. Others of us cherish our dreams as an opportunity to live lives and experiences never available in the real world. We drag slowly out of bed and carry fragments of the night into our jobs. We're the ones accused of daydreaming.

At the root of these very different personalities is the active/passive separation. Active people are always involved with the people and events around them, living externally. The passive personality lives more within itself and interacts mostly when the world forces it to.

Women have the reputation of being passive personalities. In times past, we often acted passive even if that were not our disposition because we were excluded from business, commerce, and decision

45

making. Now that men and women both have more freedom, we see that active and passive traits are not sex determined.

Active and passive personalities cannot be determined by how we spend our days. Many housewives are active women, and there are passive women holding management-level jobs, although a passive woman is more likely to be noted in the corporate structure for her talents than for her drive.

The mother of three who's head of the PTA, a volunteer working for her local city councilman, playing tennis in the afternoon and learning to throw pots at night is an example of an active energy type.

The passive worker is the one noted for her calm approach to work. She tends to ignore the actions of those around her unless they're angry with her. When her boss screams about the other workers, she calmly lights a cigarette, and continues with her report. When he tells *her* to get that report out right this minute, she may go into a panic unless reassured. Her boss is an active. Few passives rise to top positions, but most don't want to be there either. Passives temper aggression and probably are the ones who save the race from extinction, but they must be activated to be at their best. Together, active and passive personalities make the world work, but alone, each has her own set of problems in the social arena.

The Active/Passive Quiz is designed to help you assess your energy type. In the chapters to come, the specific pages on where and how to pick up a man,

I have keyed those situations where a passive woman will have an advantage or where an active woman will be most comfortable picking up a man by noting Active or Passive in parentheses at the end of the description.

In general, an "active" woman will have an easier time picking up a man. Her natural high energy helps push her to make the first move and risk rejection, but passives can also take control of their social lives if they'll just learn the basics and look for the situations marked for their personality.

Take the quiz. Mark your answers on a separate piece of paper and look for scoring instructions at the end. Please think carefully and try to answer each question with the most honest answer, not the one you would like to be true. In some cases neither answer will totally describe your reaction. If that happens try to choose the description that seems closest to what you'd do.

CHOOSE ONE

1. You're standing in line at the supermarket when, two people ahead, a man starts quarreling over the price of cereal and demands a re-ring and the manager. You:

    a. Wait it out. You're already established and what's a little extra time?

    b. Note that it looks like a long siege, grab your cart and move to another line.

2. You're seated on the bus and a twelve-year-old girl stands in front of you. The bus is crowded, with people close around you, but you notice the fly on her pants is open. You:

    a. Pretend not to notice so as not to embarrass her or yourself by drawing the attention of other passengers.

    b. Tap her arm and say, "You'd better zip up." A little embarrassment now will save her later embarrassment on the street.

3. You receive a bill from the doctor and it looks like he's charged you for a test you're sure you never had. However, you've never quite understood medical jargon and figure it could be correct. You:

    a. Pay it anyway if the charge isn't that much.

    b. Call the doctor and ask him to explain his notations.

4. You're driving down the expressway and come to the toll booth, one of those automated kind that you pitch your money into. You toss your fifty cents in the bin and one quarter tips on the edge and falls to the ground. You:

    a. Wait for the attendant to come pick it up, as the sign says to do, even as the cars pile up behind you.

    b. Get out of your car and pick it up and drop it in.

5. Your boss asks you to stay after work to type up some reports for him as a "favor" (no overtime). He's not a friend and offers no favor in return. You:

    a. Do it, since he's the boss and you don't want to risk getting fired.

    b. Tell him you have a dinner date, but for time and a half you could break it, or perhaps the reports could be done first thing in the morning.

6. At a club you sometimes frequent, you get up the nerve to ask an attractive man to dance. He accepts, and only then do you find he's a very showy dancer, lifting you in the air, spinning you around and jumping around like a madman. You:

    a. Suggest you two sit down and talk instead; you're uncomfortable acting that way in public.

    b. Pick up his style as much as possible and try to see his unusual athletics as an opportunity for some fun.

7. A new boyfriend takes you to dinner at the home of another couple, friends you've never met. After dinner, she starts clearing the table and putting the food away while the guys talk football on the couch—a subject you know nothing about. You:

    a. Stick with your boyfriend since you don't really know the woman or want to wash dishes.

    b. Pick up your plate and flatware and pitch in, talking to the woman about something you are interested in.

8. Your idea of a good summer Saturday at the beach is:

  a. Wading in the shallows, reading on your towel and getting a good tan.

  b. Body-surfing, volleyball, and talking to other bathers.

9. When you must make a decision, you:

  a. Collect all available facts and information and weigh them carefully until time's up and then make your move.

  b. Decide quickly and then concentrate all your energy on making your choice work, even if it wasn't right.

10. Traditionally, your family goes to your aunt's house for Thanksgiving dinner. Your aunt is a bad cook and her cats give you allergies. Last June you got your own apartment, but now it's November and your mother's pressing you to join the family at your aunt's. You:

  a. Go to auntie's. Life is full of obligation, tradition is important and with antihistamines her cats won't kill you.

  b. Make a reservation at a nice restaurant and tell your mom you just can't make it, no matter what she says.

11. It's Friday night. You've been invited to join some friends from work at a concert you don't want to miss. Trouble is, you got to the bank too late to cash your paycheck and you're too broke to both make the concert and eat this weekend. You:

  a. Apologize for not joining your friends, stay home and watch TV.

   b. Call up a close friend and wangle twenty
      bucks until Monday.

12. You see a folded piece of paper fall out of the
pocket of a nice-looking man walking ahead of you
on the street. You:

   a. Keep walking, it probably wasn't important
      and it's none of your business anyway.

   b. Pick it up and call to him. It may be nothing
      but you'd like to meet him.

13. Your girl friend is always late. When you decide on dinner at seven, she appears at eight, when
you meet at the theater for an eight o'clock show,
she arrives ten minutes after the movie starts. Recently you arranged to meet her on the street corner
to go shopping. She arrived twenty minutes late,
assuming that no apologies were necessary. You:

   a. Grumble. She's your friend and telling her
      how mad you are may ruin an otherwise
      good friendship.

   b. Tell her this is the third time she's been late
      in two weeks and she's not showing any re-
      spect for your friendship. You're not going
      to make any more appointments.

14. A couple you know just split up; since you
like them equally, you hope to be friendly with each.
She, however, is furious when you accept an invitation to a party from him. She thinks you're interested in him romantically and maybe were all along.
She will not tolerate your "friendship" with him if
you want to be friends with her. You:

a. Tell her you'll stay away from the party so she won't be mad, since you understand things must be hard for her. Does it matter if you're friends with him anyway?

b. Tell her she's being foolish. You like him just as you do her, and if she wants to stay friends with you, she will just have to change.

15. Your neighbor in the apartment below is giving a Saturday night party on his terrace, just below your bedroom. It's midnight and you'd like to sleep, but the noise is too much. You:

a. Turn on your light and try to read. Twelve o'clock is not late after all.

b. Open the window or call on the house phone: "Hey, could you and your guests move inside? I'm trying to sleep."

16. A man you like but don't know well invites you out to dinner on Friday night. You eagerly accept, but when he comes by, he announces he's made a reservation at a Japanese restaurant. You hate Japanese food, but want him to like you, so you:

a. Say, "Oh great" (thinking you can push the food around on your plate and eat some rice and tell him the truth when you know him better).

b. Tell him you'd planned to take him to a restaurant in your neighborhood.

17. Your current boyfriend asks if you'd like to spend next weekend with his closest friends, a couple

you can take for an evening but never a whole weekend. You think your boyfriend may be testing your loyalty, so you:

    a. Say, "Oh yes, I'd love it" and hate it.

    b. Say, "Well, I don't think I can take your friends for a *whole* weekend. I'll go for one night."

18. Your sister has asked you to read the novel she's been working on evenings for a year. She wants to know if you think it's worthy of publication. When you read the first chapter, you know she hasn't a chance. You tell her:

    a. It needs a little more work.

    b. It's lousy.

19. A job opening comes up at work. It's a better job than you currently have, paying more money. You think you may be able to handle it but aren't quite sure. You:

    a. Work very hard and let your superiors see you doing it, so that they'll notice you and offer you the promotion.

    b. Apply for the opening and guarantee them you know the work, even if you don't.

20. You leave your apartment to go to work and find a large, dirty man asleep between the outer door and the locked security doors. He fills the small space and you can't get around him. You live alone and he looks mean. You:

    a. Go back in your apartment, call the super and ask him to do something about it.

   b. Say, "Come on, let me get by. You shouldn't be in here," and try to awaken him.

SCORING

Thirteen or more A answers indicates a passive bent to your personality. You're ambiguous about making decisions, partly because you want to be liked and hate hurting others' feelings. You prefer to move through life with as few battles as possible, always looking for a way to keep everyone happy before taking a stand. When they get to know you, people are likely to describe you as a nice, thoughtful friend. Before they know you they may think you're distant or even unfriendly because you wait for them to initiate friendship. If you live in California you'll be called laid back. None of this is a reflection on your intelligence. You will often have a thorough, methodical approach to your business that astounds active personalities. Left alone, you can also transfer your daydreams to art, but beware the opinions of others; you're too inclined to take advice, even when it's bad.

Approaching a man is hard for you, as is approaching a salesclerk for help or a waitress to get your check, but since you are most comfortable when you know you will make others happy, I have included approaches in the upcoming chapters that will put you at ease by flattering or helping the men you wish to meet. Look for the Passive marking following these scenarios, but don't feel you can't use another approach if it feels right. As you pick up more men, you may find yourself becoming more of an Active in your social life.

Thirteen or more B answers indicate an active personality. You enjoy your many friends but aren't afraid of turning them into enemies if they annoy you. You're willing to take the kind of chances that sometimes land you on top, but your quick decisions can also lead to bad ventures and unwise relationships. You're the one who decides to take that poor shivering teenager in off the street only to discover he's a junkie who walks off with your stereo as soon as you turn your back. You can make so many friends that if you're not careful they all become acquaintances, since you don't have the time to spend on deeper relationships. Men usually like you, but you have problems in picking them up because you often overwhelm them with too much too soon. If you live in California, they think you're from New York. Look for the scenarios marked Active in upcoming chapters. They will suit your outgoing personality. If you give the guys a little breathing room, you'll have all the interesting men you want.

Equal As and Bs. You're balanced, integrated. There will probably be a time and place when any approach in this book feels right for you. Remember: Active approaches take more initiative but get faster results. Passive approaches are slower, but easier to back away from. Pick, choose and experiment.

7

The Basics of Approach

You've prepared your mental attitude, you've listened to the men and you've learned not to listen to some women. Your thoughts are positive, your tension is working for you, you're all dressed up and know you look your best. You are ready, really ready, to go out and pick up a man. Good. Now here is how to do it.

Be honest. You'll find sample opening sentences in the coming scenarios—"lines," as they've been called. Understand that they are only examples to be adapted to your own interests and personality. Don't memorize them. Draw instead on the moment for a *similar* comment. Never invent a persona; you and your real life are never too dull to intrigue the man you approach. Example: Pretending you're interested in auto mechanics to make a mechanic like you can lead to some pretty grim and grimy hours in the garage. It's more important to be interested in the *fact* that he's interested in car mechanics. You can say, "I don't know a thing about car repair. I've never even known a mechanic. Tell me what you like about your work." You've stayed honest and avoided helping him rebuild a transmission.

At times I will suggest an opening designed to startle a man, catch him off guard, and engage him in conversation without the awkward moments of introducing yourself and fumbling for a reason why you're introducing yourself. An example is saying, "It must be beautiful in San Diego today," when you're standing on a rainy street in Toledo, Ohio. Instead of appraising you and wondering if you're a woman he wants to date, he'll think, "San Diego?" and say, "Why San Diego?" allowing you to comfortably describe the beauty of San Diego at just this time of year. These lines are positive and designed to put you at ease and carry you over the initial fear of approach, but they will only succeed in giving you confidence if you really know your subject. If you start with a lie and construct an elaborate fabrication he'll begin to see the holes in your story and he'll think you a little crazy. As long as you're entertaining him with warmth and special knowledge, he's intrigued.

Exercise humor. The seriousness of women is legendary and you will be raised immediately in a man's eyes if you can laugh at his jokes and *deliver your own.* Most male-to-male interchange is in the form of jokes, ribs and friendly insults. Just watch some buddies at a baseball game if you've never noticed this before. A man really will take you more seriously as a person if you can laugh. Open with a funny comment on what's going on around you (anything but a slice at him) and you've made a good impression. Laughing and smiling as you talk communicates that you're a fun person to be with and can disguise the nervousness you feel. Practicing a humorous approach to life can make your life happier. There's no effort lost here.

Never play dumb to pick up a man. It sounds like a reminder too antiquated to warrant inclusion here, but I still see women slipping into outdated attitudes when faced with an attractive stranger. Perhaps it's because so many well-intentioned older people still caution, "Don't act so smart, you'll scare him away." This ploy is senseless today. If you can scare a man by showing more intelligence than he, would you want to spend an evening with him? Think of a weekend alone with him in a remote cabin. If it's impossible to imagine, he's better gone. Think too of the options you present a man when you show him an empty head. All he's left to focus on are your face and body, and I assure you he will judge these more harshly if he must consider introducing a stupid woman to his friends. He'll have to convince them he's with you for your looks, so they'd better be spectacular.

The men I've spoken to list friendliness, humor, interest in them, attractiveness and intelligence as the traits they find most appealing. No one said dumb as a post.

Try to approach a man when both of you are alone. If you're with girl friends they may tease you or try to discourage you with all the old myths (see chapter 5), and if he's with buddies they'll do that and more. Men in groups act very differently than a man alone does. Showing an interest in one member of a group is an invitation for his jealous buddies to denigrate your intentions to assuage their feelings of rejection. If they're young they'll tell him you must have hot pants, and he'll respond to you as if you do, for his buddies' benefit. You'll be more comfortable when you can avoid judgement of this kind. This is why sporting events and neighborhood bars, though teeming with men, are bad pick-up spots. Wherever men hang out with their cronies, you'll be intruding if you try to break up the gang, no matter how much the individual man really would like to meet you.

If you really want company to go to a party or a bar, try a platonic male friend. It says you're desirable, one man already finds you so, and that you're not desperate for companionship when you start talking to another man. Don't worry about encouraging social competition. It exists in all parties and bars, and while I've never quite liked it, I'd rather use it than suffer from it. When you begin talking to another man, just reassure him that he needn't worry about your friend, that there's nothing between you. You'll seem still more intriguing, and if neither you nor your friend meets anyone, you'll have someone there to talk to and ride home with.

I've had several close male friends in the last six years with whom I've prowled bars and attended parties I never would have dared go to otherwise. When you want to explore a club in a bad section of town, or go to a party where you'll know no one, think of your male friends. The more men you develop as platonic friends, the more comfortable you'll be speaking to any man.

Ask a new man to lunch. There's less pressure for romance and making a commitment. Lunch can be turned into a very memorable seduction if you want it that way because he'll never be expecting it, but it can also be a friendly conclusion to a false start, with no real hard feelings, if you discover you're not compatible. If you just want a slow build to intimacy, it's a good prelude to a more formal evening date, and if his feelings seem to be racing ahead of your own, split the bill. When you share, he can never feel he's invested in you and thus get pushy.

Don't pick him up and then hand him the reins. Continue controlling your life as a pick-up moves into dating. Start by exchanging phone numbers, don't just wait for him to ask for yours. If you feel that he is the person you would like to see a new film with, call him up and tell him exactly that, with no excuses or apologies for taking the initiative. Treat him as you would any other friend and he will become a friend.

Be observant. Watch the man you're interested in before you do anything. By examining his clothing, actions, surroundings, and mood (nervous, relaxed, anticipatory), you can often know what he's thinking. Then *speak his thoughts.* Is he tapping his foot, glancing at his watch, dressed well and staring up the street? He's probably waiting for a car or cab. Furthermore, it's late and he's worrying about missing something. Observing this, you say, "Running late? These cabs are never around when you need them." Because you've spoken his thoughts, he's apt to launch right into conversation with you. Another example: Is he walking down the street slowly, peering at doorways, backing up and walking on, looking a bit nervous? Say, "What address are you looking for?" By observing you knew he was lost, you can speak to him easily because you are offering legitimate aid.

The more you watch people, the more aware you will become of subtler thoughts, and you will know how to speak them and surprise a man with your insight, making him receptive to you.

Look him in the eyes. A woman can pick a man up without saying a word if she uses her eyes effectively. It's surprising how uncomfortable most women are looking into a man's eyes with bold interest. Practice. Men find such boldness exciting, indicative of strength and spirit. If you look at a man reading a paper with frank interest, he'll feel your gaze and look up. If you can keep your eyes on his at that first awkward moment, he will talk to you.

Get his name and use it. We tingle a little when we hear our names. Maybe it's self love, but a man will feel happier, and more relaxed with you, if you use his name. He will listen to your voice when you speak it, and if he hears affection he will return affection. In an increasingly depersonalized time, that little island of warmth will set a loving tone for whatever friendship follows.

Give him an honest compliment. Something attracted you to a man if you're approaching him, so put it into simple, sincere words and say them without embarrassment. We all enjoy knowing that we've been noticed and appreciated, but at the same time we all wonder whether we really are worthy of appreciation. When you tell a man that he has great hair, he's happy to meet you and more apt to project his most positive side.

Smile. If the man you've been watching suddenly meets your gaze, smile. Just like holding your eyes on his, many women find it hard to smile and be overtly warm to men they don't know well. It's probably because we're cautioned so often about the dangers of unknown men. From the time we're old enough to remember, our parents are warning us not to speak to strange men, not to look at strange men, not even to acknowledge their existence, for fear we'll loose the beast in them. I remember a talk my father had with me when I was fourteen. He told me that young women were filled with warm maternal feelings that would eventually prepare us for motherhood. Young men, on the other hand, were full of sexual longings, longings so strong that they obscured any kind of real love and that men didn't feel love like women did until months or years after marriage, when their longings had been satisfied.

What he meant to do was discourage me from making love until I was married, but all I felt afterward was a profound sadness that he had not loved my mother when he married her. Fortunately, my first lover was kind and loving and dispelled this myth immediately, helping me to start feeling good about men.

If you can remind yourself when you're looking at a man that he is just another human being hoping for love and acceptance, smiling will come easily; and when you realize that a man can't trap you just because you're friendly, you can enjoy his smile in return.

Stand close to him. Don't lean on him or trap him in a corner, but come near and you create a sense of intimacy. He'll feel that you wouldn't recoil if he touched you. Then when you do speak, he's expecting it and feels less awkward, meaning you'll feel more relaxed too.

Share. If you have a bag of candy, nuts, popcorn,

and see a man watching you eat, offer him some. Smiling and holding out the bag is enough to start. Food is the physical pleasure we're freest to indulge in and discuss, and most men will appreciate your offering to share pleasure with them.

Send a drink to him. When you see a man in a restaurant or bar sitting alone and he already has a drink glass on the table, there is no greater way to make an instant impression than sending him a drink. If a man's ever done it to you, you know it's a very elegant introduction. It's also a chicken's delight. You make your deal through a middleman (the waiter) to whom you say simply, "Send that gentleman another of what he's having." The waiter will not censure you, and part of the deal is that he point out the sender to the recipient of the gift. When your man looks up at you, raise your own drink in toast. Expect a powerful reaction.

Have personal business cards printed. Even if you have no business worth promoting on a card, they are an excellent entrée and eliminate the hurdle of asking for his number or waiting for him to ask for yours. When you tell him your name, you present him with a card at the same time. Many small printing companies specialize in business cards; you can find them in the Yellow Pages in any town. Your name and phone number, in neat script or block letters is sufficient, though you can often make your card more complete. A secretary can add "transcription services" without lying.

A bold woman can get reactions from a funny message, like "Leisure Coordinator," meaning she's really unemployed, but you should avoid openly sexual messages. You'll make him more uncomfortable than interested.

Here then are the hows of picking up men. You'll never need them all at one time, but two or three will get the response you want, while keeping you as cool as possible. With the next chapter, we'll begin exploring where and when and what to say.

8

The Kindness of Strangers

For poor Blanche DuBois in a *A Streetcar Named Desire*, the kindness of strangers was a deadly lure, a helpless Southern belle's way of surviving with negligible skills and no inclination to dirty her feminine paws with real labor. While men may have helped Blanche survive for a time, it's your kindness *to* men that will help you meet one.

When you're faced with a new school, a new job or a new relationship, you're most likely to seek strength in comfortable old behavior. That behavior may not be the best way to live at all times, but the important thing is that it makes *you* better able to cope in making a big change. In that same vein, a good way to start picking up men is with the assertive behavior we feel most comfortable with.

Women are raised to be helpful and giving; it's part of the old preparation for motherhood, so there's no easier way for a woman to assert herself than by stepping forward to help another. Helping is the key to all the scenarios in this chapter. Many of the approaches can even be started by saying, "Can I help?" While feminists may criticize and say this is the kind of behavior women are trying to get away from, I say that some things are better taken in steps than leaps. When you see a man struggling, why not offer aid? When it develops into a night out or a relationship, you've learned to be more assertive in one easy pleasant lesson. And we're becoming a world so short on kindness. As others shy from involvement, you can make a strong impression on a man just by being helpful.

Here are ten ways to meet strangers. They'll all make your first impression a positive one without giving him the impression that you're offering to be his servant. There are also ten favors that you can do for men you've met but never quite been able to connect with.

One final word: You will notice that I've not included favors like mending his clothes, doing his laundry, taking on typing or running errands. When you let yourself in for this kind of aid, you can find it becoming a chore. A true pick-up kindness keeps you together or brings you together. It's never a job without pay.

You'll find your Active and Passive notation in parentheses after each of the approaches.

1. Walking down the street you see a man moving into a new home and struggling with an un-

gainly piece of furniture. Step up and say, "Excuse me, do you need some help carrying that coffee table up the stairs?"

Moving is not only hard work, it's emotionally traumatic. He's leaving a familiar neighborhood, maybe some friends, and your joking and friendliness will boost his spirits while you get that table up the stairs. Why should you work so hard for a stranger? It's good for your legs for one thing, and shared suffering, no matter how slight, brings people together. Why not help him move the rest if you have the time? You'll both be hungry or thirsty from your work, and he'll be glad to get away from all those boxes and furniture to have a meal with you. (Active)

Keep your ear open when a friend mentions getting a group together to help someone move. You hear it all the time and you can reasonably ask how many will be there, to help with the heavy work. If there are a lot of people, it's almost like a party, and with a well-placed suggestion it can turn into one afterwards, with you still reaping the benefits of shared "suffering." (Passive)

2. At the holiday season, you always see men struggling through stores with packages, but you'll see them at other times too, as in sporting goods departments where they'll have a long way to walk to get that new sleeping bag and camp stove out to the street. Offer to help him carry something out to a cab or his car. If you see a bag slipping from his

stack, it's even better; reach out to catch it and if he protests, say, "Let me help. I know you're over-loaded." He only protests because he doesn't want to impose. At car or cab you can say "Going up-town?" or wherever you're headed. If he hasn't offered you a lift already, he'll be glad to repay your kindness by giving you a ride and a chance to introduce yourself. (Active)

3. How many times have you seen a man trans-ferring several suitcases or boxes to the street to be picked up by a car or cab? It's a tough situation for him because he has to chance leaving his be-longings unprotected on the street while he goes in for another load, unless you, passing by, can muster a simple, "Want me to watch those?" If he hesi-tates, reassure him you're not a thief by giving him your card. He'll know your name and number right away, and when he has everything transferred out-side, ask for his card or number. He'll probably have to go off with his boxes but you can always say, "How about a drink when you get back?" Shy women usually find it easier to arrange a future meeting than go off with a man they've just met. (Passive)

4. Open the door for that overburdened man in the store or office building. When he looks up, startled by your courtesy, give him a blinding smile and say, "My pleasure." He'll have to say something! Lighting cigarettes, opening doors, and pulling out a chair for a man, doing everything, in short, that

gentlemen once had to do for ladies, gets a man's attention fast and charms him more than a little. When you do it as a kindness or even jokingly, he won't think you're making a political statement and will love the turnabout. (Passive)

5. Take a walk through the men's wear department next time you go shopping. When you see an attractive man looking at sunglasses, stop and tell him they really look good. Then examine the rack and pick another pair, saying, "Can I see how these would look?" and urge him to try them on. Men dress to look good for women and most will appreciate a woman's opinions before they buy. "I never imagined anyone would look so good in that," is the sort of comment that makes him feel good about himself and you. If you're in a department store with a restaurant, ask him if he's ever tried it, and if he'd like to. On the heels of a compliment it's unlikely that he'll say no. (Active)

6. Have you ever watched young men at the meat counter in the grocery store? Most men new to cooking don't know about different cuts or cooking methods, and they're always looking for something they can broil or fry. When you see an interesting looking man who seems to be having trouble, ask if you can help him find the cut he wants. "Are you looking for a good steak?" usually suffices. Show him which ones are tender and tell him how you like it fixed, with some sautéed mushrooms, and a little red wine, perhaps. When he says he's a plainer

cook than that (he wouldn't have needed your help if he wasn't), offer to come show him your way. It's a move for actives, unless a passive can describe a meal so well that he asks her to come over and teach him. (Active)

7. If you know something about wine, you can transfer the last hint to the liquor store. See a man wandering around the racks looking overwhelmed by the selection? Make a gentle suggestion. If you know a few good wines, don't be afraid; he doesn't want to spend all day looking for something to drink. Your approach can be as simple as "Ever tried this? Someone turned me on to this right in this store and it's really good." Passing on favors is a great tradition and this one can be followed with, "If you need help drinking it . . ." (Passive)

8. If you live in a major city, you must see professional dog walkers occasionally. Many are actors or students or artists or other young men needing extra cash. No matter what they are, I've seldom seen any who weren't interesting looking, and struggling along with five lurching dogs, they can always use a little kindness. Fall in beside him and say, "Need help?" holding out your hand to take a leash or two. Pretty easy, and the conversation will be too, with both the dogs and their owners to talk about. He'll walk them at about the same time every day, so you can be there to help the next day if it takes that long for you to invite him for coffee afterward. (Passive)

9. How often have you seen a man fixing his car in the driveway, lying underneath and groping for his tools? If the part of him protruding from under the wheels looks good, why not hand him the tool he's feeling for or ask which he wants. He'll stick his head out pretty fast to see who you are, and if you're sitll interested, ask if he'd like you to help by handing him tools. You can get a doctor/nurse game going, "Scalpel, scalpel. Wrench, wrench." When you get thirsty, offer to bring him back a drink too. Not a bad way to make a friend and spend a lazy summer afternoon. (Active)

10. Tell that nice-looking man on the street that his pockets are inside out. Tell him there's a piece of paper clinging to his cuff. I've even been known to inform a man that his fly's at half mast. But very *nicely.* "Oh, watch out, don't step in the _____!" is another valuable kindness you can do for a man on the street. Don't snicker at his expense; just tell him there's something you think he'd want to know about and that you want to spare him embarrassment. Then fall in stride and tell him something embarrassing that once happened to you. You'll soon have him laughing at your story and on his way to sitting down and talking a little more with you in a more relaxed atmosphere. (Active)

Now for that man you've never been able to get anything going with. He may be the friend of a friend, a man you see at parties or someone who works in another office in your building. You see him all the time, he's friendly and yet he doesn't make the move. Here's how *you* can.

1. You see him standing by the elevator and he looks tense, maybe he's rolling his head around or rubbing his neck. Walk up, touch him lightly on the shoulders and say, "Want a massage?" Start kneading before he makes up his mind and the answer will be yes. Ask what made him so tense, get him talking about what bothers him and empathize, saying that some of those things bother you too, all the time squeezing the tensions out of his muscles, leaning into him a little, and talking in a soothing voice. This healing, nonaggressive body contact will make him wonder how your touch would feel under different circumstances. Suggest a drink to complete his relaxation. (Active)

2. Many men don't know where to go for a haircut anymore. Barbershops are disappearing and styling salons are intimidating and alien to a no-frills man. When you see his hair getting shaggy, ask if he'd like a cheap cut, provided you have the skill. If he's like my husband, stepson or any of a dozen men I know, he'll be grateful to have the job taken care of so easily. A haircut is not as sensual as a massage, but you can go to his house for it and massage his scalp, compliment him on his hair and ruffle it, and make him feel just about as good.

You've also saved him time and trouble, and it's only natural for him to offer you food or drink and some pleasant conversation after the clip. (Passive)

3. Nothing touches a man more than the women who will help him when he's sick. Call him up and tell him you're bringing him some chicken soup, even if it's just Campbell's. Offer to go out to get him some staples, or again, give him a nice, relaxing massage. (Passive)

4. An unusual remedy will also hearten a sick man. If it has to be cooked on his stove and tastes good, it's an ideal remedy. Make him some warm brandy with cream and honey or that tea from Chinatown that's supposed to kill all evils known to mankind, especially when you add whiskey to it. Use your nurturing talents, but remind him that you're not Mom by dressing in something a little more daring than you would usually wear. An extra button left open is enough. Just by being there in a bad moment you've forged a bond. (Passive)

5. Noticing that a man has a new suit, shirt, shoes, haircut, hat or briefcase and complimenting him on it, or them, will make him aware of how much you look at him. And if you see and compliment him on some very small change, an expensive new key chain, say, that nobody else notices, it's truly flattering and will make him start wondering why he's never looked at you more closely. He'll begin noticing you, and when he starts returning compliments it'll be hard to keep a friendship from blossoming.

After all, you're both admiring each other so much. (Active/Passive)

6. When you run into him and see that he's depressed, insist he come have a drink to cheer up. Men do this with casual acquaintances all the time, so why shouldn't you? It shows concern for his happiness and lets you be the one to restore his happy state. This works so well you may have to slow him down if you don't want to spend the whole night with him. (Active)

7. You can use essentially the same approach when you know he has something to celebrate. Say he tells you he just made his first door-to-door dictionary sale. You can make it a big deal worthy of celebration with your enthusiasm. Say, "That's wonderful! Congratulations! Let me buy you a drink!" Just as above, you're sweeping him up for a good reason, and he'll be happy to go along. (Active)

8. Find out when his birthday is and send him a card. If he's over thirty, you can write a funny message inside about looking on the bright side and how he's only mellowing with age like a good wine. This can cheer him on a rough day and, again, let him know you think about him more than he knew. (Passive)

9. If you were both at a party, or any kind of event where he was not at his best, send him a funny, friendly souvenir relating to the occasion. Example: If he was the one who got sunburned at the beach party, send him a postcard of a bright red Maine

lobster, saying, "Seems someone snuck up on you with a camera when you were sunbathing. I've laid in a big bottle of Bactine for the next party." Or if he got tipsy and silly at the Christmas party, send him a cut-out-and-fold-together lamp shade of your own design. Draw it on a sheet of cardboard with funny-but-friendly instructions. He's embarrassed about what happened and maybe wonders what his friends are thinking of him, so when you send him a souvenir telling him you thought it was all a great joke and you like him for being so human, he'll feel better about his behavior and very good about you. (Passive)

10. This last may seem daring, but it still involves the mail so it can be done by anyone. Scan the sex magazines at your local store. Look for cover lines that relate to something nonsexual that he's interested in. When you find one with a good article, buy the issue and cut out the story (those photos and words on the back of the pages identify where it came from). Mail it to him with a short note saying you knew he was interested in the subject and thought he might like the article. Nothing more. He'll look on the backs of the pages and it will make him think that he really doesn't know much about you. You'll arouse his curiosity about more than your reading habits. (Active/Passive)

See how easy it is to be kind? And one of the nicest things about starting a friendship with a kind act is that no matter how things progress, you have been established as a woman of good instincts, and he is likely to treat you with the same kindness you showed him. It makes me think of my husband Bobby.

Bobby has always gone out of his way to help his friends and even strangers, if they need him. He's taken photos for little or free, he's helped dozens move, he's loaned cameras and worked weekends and consoled hysterical pals on the phone at three o'clock in the morning. A lot of people tell him he's crazy to do so much, but our house is full of beautiful gifts made by these friends, and any time Bobby needs a favor himself there are dozens ready to help.

Sometimes kindness takes a little trouble or muscle but the return in genuine friendships is invaluable.

9

Looking Good

"What I want to know is something I can say to a man to make him love me before he takes a good look below my neck. Men love bodies, and even if I exercised all day, every day, I'd never be centerfold material." That from a woman in her early thirties who dresses beautifully, makes up with care and smiles so much that few people do look below her neck, though there's nothing wrong with what's down there.

The biggest complaint that women have about the kind of magazine I work for is that they create unreasonable standards of beauty. We recently ran a questionnaire in *Oui* for our women readers asking how often they buy the magazine and what their main interest in it is. Over 90 percent of the women said the first thing they do with the magazine is compare themselves to the models. Some also noted that they did this to make themselves feel good, because they stacked up well against the competition.

Well, I'd like to say to all women that there is no

competition. Men's magazines are fantasies, the women in them are fantasies—real people away from the camera, but fantasies on paper. Of course, I'm not saying there aren't women who are luckier than others in the genetic jackpot. Where most of the population draws two or three features that mesh with current standards of beauty, a few women are given ten. We who work at men's magazines work hard and continuously to find these women, but it's no secret that even the beauties we find must be further perfected through careful posing, makeup, concealing clothing and draping, expert lighting and choice of camera angle. After all that, only a handful of photos out of the hundreds taken will ever be deemed fit for publication, and those may be even further perfected through retouching. That's all because fantasy gains its impact from transcending reality. If Superman had no impossible muscles and special powers he wouldn't be a hero. Women in men's magazines are the Supermen of sexual fantasy; great fifteen-minute flights of fancy, but nothing anyone ever expects to meet in the bank. Unfortunately most men won't admit that they use men's magazines like grown-up comic books, and women are left to worry that there's more to them than a few moments of vicariously leaping high buildings.

The best way for me to prove that men don't use centerfold women as their standards of beauty for flesh-and-blood women is to turn to my mail. Photos of "real" women submitted by readers are the most popular new feature in men's magazines in ten years. Almost every magazine features these "Real People" photos in some way, and many many more photos than can be used come in the mail, sent usually with a testimonial letter from husband or boyfriend, reading something like this:

"My wife/girl friend is more beautiful than any of the girls in your magazine. We felt her beauty would be appreciated by your readers so we took these photos. Her hobbies are ————, ————, and ———— and she works as a ————. In addition, she is the most wonderful woman I've ever known."

And when we look at the thoroughly average but happy and well loved lady beaming out of the Polaroids, we know it's the last sentence in her man's letter that makes him sincere in the others.

You see, all perceptions of real beauty are dependent on love, admiration and affection. Women have always admitted this, but men have been painted as satyrs for so long that their susceptibility to a great personality is underestimated. Unless you are very under- or overweight, your small breasts, big breasts, droopy breasts, wide waist, loose tummy, full bottom, big thighs, skinny calves, thick ankles or big feet—whatever you have decided is imperfect, uncenterfoldish, about your figure—is really not going to matter as much to him as it does to you, *if* he enjoys your company. One reason is that he sees your self-image projected over your body. If you're acting confident and strong, he's most aware of those parts of your body that back up that picture, and if you feel sexy and seductive, he sees only curves and soft skin. It's only if you project self-loathing that he will concentrate on the parts you hate.

But there is an even simpler reason why he won't judge you as you judge yourself: he's insecure too. He's scrutinized his body and decided that he has narrow shoulders, a hairy back, thin arms, small hands, hairless chest, beer belly, love handles, flat bottom, small penis, short legs, fat bottom, skinny legs crooked toes, etc.

We all look with some dismay at our bodies and worry that we're imperfect which is why when we're being honest with ourselves, we realize that the last thing we really want is someone so perfect that they make our imperfections glaring by comparison. Ever dated a perfectly handsome guy? I've been out with a couple of male-model candidates and the anxiety was awful. I even came to resent their nice looks.

As Alison, a lively record company rep tells it, "I'd always had dates, but they were normal guys, guys that I felt equal to. When I got my job with the record company, I was all of a sudden thrown in contact with lots of really great-looking men— musicians hoping to get signed and some who were already signed. I thought I was in heaven when they started taking me to clubs and stuff, but then I heard a few people hinting that they were just with me to butter me up. A couple of gossips is all it took to make me take a good look at them and a good look at me and lose all my self-confidence. I got so inhibited in bed I'd want the lights out when I undressed so they wouldn't see my fat thighs. When I had a couple of dreams about taking off my clothes, and the guy just getting up and walking out without a word, I started looking around for those nice, normal guys again."

Sure we want nice-looking dates, but when they have no flaws, sometimes there's nothing to attach affection to. You can be awed or aroused by a perfect chin, but it's the crooked nose that makes him an individual and makes you feel misty and warm. And though men make much of *commenting* on female beauty, those perfected centerfold girls aren't even on their lists of date possibilities.

"But men love boobies, they *do*," complains Joan Rivers, and small-breasted women everywhere lament, "Yeah, she's right; even if they don't want us perfect they want us chesty." You must know, however, that there are many wonderful, desirable men who prefer small breasts, and that the reason there are so many small-breasted women is because men married women with small breasts who passed on the trait to their daughters.

When I asked men if they would pass up a woman whom they liked in other ways just because her breasts were small, most replied with some form of "Don't be ridiculous," "What are you talking about?" or "Do you really think we're that shallow?"

But yes, those same men will ogle large breasts, will compliment them, will joke about them, and a few will even make the comments to large-breasted women that make those women wish they had breasts more like the average. Though there are many theories on why American men are so breast conscious, my experience in making products to catch male attention, i.e., men's magazines, makes me think our national breast awareness was raised to where it is now by advertising.

Forty years ago, you couldn't publish a photo of a naked woman legally in the U.S., yet advertisers were well aware of the power of sex to catch a consumer's attention. Men were the shoppers with buying power back then, so the advertisers looked for ways to add the image of female sex to their pitches. They knew a pretty girl sold products, so how about a sexy girl?

Fine, but you couldn't go too far. You couldn't show a photo of a girl's crotch, even clothed, next to a car without being censored. It was also hard to get away with showing a fanny—too blatant. That left legs and breasts, and legs did have a great heyday in the forties, but more and more advertisers saw that breasts were the ultimate way to sell sex. It was perfectly innocent to have a girl's smiling face in your ad, and if just below that face there was a very large breast outline, the women suggested sex without showing any skin at all. Then cleavage became legal, so the competition was switched to showing as much cleavage as possible. A bigger breast gave more cleavage, and everyone interested in selling something to men looked for bigger and bigger breasts to show men more and more of the only legal expanse of female erogenous zone. And since the implication of the ads was that buying the product would win a man this sexy, pliant woman, big breasts came to be associated with high sex drive. (After all, why else would a beautiful woman throw herself at the buyer just for picking the right brand of car wax?)

Thus, to my mind, was born the Big Breast Boom, and recent studies show that college students today still believe that large-breasted women are more promiscuous and less intelligent.

So while you small-breasted women may envy the attention lavished on larger breasts, consider the stigma those women must battle. Women with large breasts can learn to handle the jokes and suggestive comments by considering that they usually come from men's sexual anxiety—men who may fear they can't measure up to your supposed high sex drive and try to prove their prowess or even scare you away with dirty comments. The more straightforward and nonflirty you are in the initial moments with a new man, the quicker he'll calm down and see past your chest.

And small-breasted women, never assume that a

man who admires larger breasts will get no pleasure from yours. He may just be a looker and talker, but in any case, he would much rather stroke your warm, soft smaller breast than watch ten Loni Andersons jiggle across a TV soundstage a thousand miles away. The body and breast that looks the best is the one cuddling up next to him.

How it gets next to him, as was said before, is dependent on words, attitude and presentation. Words and attitude are covered elsewhere in the book. Presentation breaks down into clothing, hair and makeup, and body language.

PRESENTATION

Men are not very fashion conscious. They are essentially immune to designer trends and unimpressed by labels. Some men go so far as to hint that fashion is a conspiracy to hide everything they love about women. No matter how much lip service men pay to equality between the sexes, men like women to dress in ways that enhance their femininity.

It would be very easy to say "buy this, don't buy that," but what you will be comfortable wearing depends a great deal on where you live. The best general advice I can give you is to focus on your best asset, then make your outfit a frame for that feature. If you have a small waist, accent it with a cinched belt and a loose blouse. If your legs are good, show them in slit skirts or summer cutoffs. Put the darkest or dullest colors over your worst feature and keep the bright or light shades over the best. To know more specific styles that men in your area appreciate, choose a local role model. Many women copy styles out of magazines, but watching a woman in your own town with an enviable social life will give you a much better idea of what will work for you.

Makeup tastes are much more general than clothing styles, as makeup itself falls in only two broad categories: disguise and enhancement. Theatrical makeup is disguise, as is much of the evening makeup described in high-fashion magazines. Using makeup to turn yourself into another person is fun, challenging and a great big turnoff to most men. Men like the other approach, which is flattering when you consider that enhancement means making the most of your real looks. Men don't want you to hide behind a mask and they don't want you to pretend to be someone you're not. A man wants you to be as straight with him as you want him to be with you, and if you just accent the natural colors, shadows and lines of your face, he'll think you far prettier than that geisha in *Vogue*.

Aside from a woman's eyes, hair has always been a key asset in attracting men, and thick, loose, healthy hair appeals to almost any man. Hair color is important to some men, blond being a favorite, but most men will state immediately that their preference applies to *natural* color, and a less than perfectly bleached blonde loses out to a natural brunette.

Good professional hair coloring can be undetectable and is then as appealing to men as natural hair.

Of the men I spoke to, 80 percent preferred longer hair, shoulder length or below, but they stressed that long or short, the most important consideration was movement. A head full of short bouncy curls was considered more attractive than a teased and sprayed long shag, and though the men associated elaborate hair styles and artificial color with overt sexiness, almost none expressed an interest in seeing these styles adopted by women they'd date.

What all this really adds up to is that when a man looks at a woman, he wants to see a woman. He wants her to look clean, healthy, friendly, sexy enough to give him the spark, but human, so that he can relax with her and expose his own humanness. He also likes to see that she has confidence in her looks and personality. That's the second part of presentation.

The body language of pick up is simply presenting yourself at your best. You want to project confidence, so you stand straight. Recognition of yourself as a sexually attractive woman is expressed by pulling your shoulders back, comfortably, not stiffly, to lift your breasts and rib cage. To stay relaxed, you choose something to do with your hands. Crossing your arms makes you look a bit stern, as does resting your hands on your hips with elbows cocked to the sides, but if your jacket is long, and the pockets low, one hand can reside in a pocket, with the other available for gesturing. Avoid two hands in the pockets, however, it makes you look trapped. A shoulder bag is a great anchor for one hand; let it rest loosely on top of the bag, not clutching the strap unless you suspect the man you've approached is a purse snatcher.

Sometimes when I'm speaking to someone famous who makes me really nervous, I'll hold something in one hand that I can fondle to release tension. A coin, a bead, a poker chip or guitar pick is fine, as long as it has a smooth, soothing surface to rub. The few times I've been caught using this tranquilizer, I simply explained what it was and why I was using it and nothing worse than an interesting discussion of relaxing techniques ever resulted.

After your hands, consider how you stand. Do you put your weight on one leg, thrusting your hip out at an abrupt angle? If you also put a hand on that hip, you have your classic streetwalker pose. Not too inviting, as it makes you look tough and sexually aggressive. Better to stand with your weight on both feet, knees not quite locked (locking your knees, holding them stiffly straight, can shut off the blood flow to the lower leg, causing you to tire quickly). You can arch your back just a little in this stance, pushing your buttocks out as you pull in your tummy. When you put all these tips together you have the female body presented at its most beautiful, what I call optimum posture. When we instruct a model to assume this pose, here's what we say:

shoulders back; chest out; legs straight; tummy in; back arched; and push that tushy out just a little.

Run those reminders through your mind as you walk up to a man and you will show him the most confident, attractive self possible. A model once told me of a man who approached her on the street while she was walking in her optimum posture. "He said that in his country they would say I 'walked like the captain of a ship,'" she said. "He explained that it meant I walked with pride and that it was a great compliment, one not often given to a woman."

I like that expression "captain of a ship." A captain has complete confidence, and that positive self-image is what you'd like to show the man you're approaching, even if you're trembling a little inside —especially if you're trembling inside. The way you walk not only reflects your self-image, but affects it. When you stand, sit and walk straight, with chest thrust out, your confidence increases almost immediately. When you walk in the same way with a little roll to your hips, you feel confident *and* sexy, and the stares of men will prove that what you feel is projected.

10

The Time Factor

When you think of where to pick up a man, what is the first image that comes to mind? Is it dark and noisy, festooned with hanging plants, cowboy hats, posters or art reproductions? Is there a band or jukebox playing and a tinkle of wet glassware? Is it stocked with men and women vying for attention?

The singles bar is a great institution, but it surprised me how many women, when I told them I was writing this book, immediately responded, "Gee, that's great, but I hate singles bars." It seems *pick up* and *singles bar* have become synonymous and not with the best connotation. Look at the *American Heritage Dictionary* definition of pick up: "To make casual acquaintance with, usually in anticipation of sexual relations." That does describe the action of a singles bar pretty succinctly, but when we speak of pick up here it just means *to initiate friendship,* or going up to a man you find attractive and starting a conversation. There are any number of places it can happen and many ways that the conversation can proceed, ranging from "See you around," or "How about lunch tomorrow?" to "Let's go to your place."

The man you pick up will have his own ideas of what he wants from the encounter, but you can conduct your pick-up in a way that will lead to the results you want.

Perhaps the most important step in controlling your pick-up is the time of day when you approach a man. Let's take the evening and that singles bar as an example. When a man goes out at night to a singles bar, he's thinking of having sex. He also hopes to meet a woman whom he'll like and will enjoy being with, but his foremost thought is the possibility for quick gratification. Otherwise he might go to the opera. So if you consider his thoughts when you think of going to a singles bar, you'll only go on nights when you too are looking for adventure and will never feel insulted because he doesn't want to wait for the third date.

Now think of mornings. Is it hard to think of picking up a man on the way to work? It's also hard for him to believe that you would pick him up with sexual intent at that early hour, making mornings an ideal time to meet a man for a gradually developing relationship. Another plus for mornings is that your time is usually limited, you have to go to work, he has errands to run, so if you're shy or nervous about picking up a man, mornings force you to make it short.

And what of afternoons? You've already learned that it's best to pick up a man who is alone, and public places throng with single, solitary men in the late afternoon. After work or on weekends single men have no responsibilities, and they often use their time for unplanned entertainment. That means they are in the right frame of mind to meet a woman interested in a little conversation, and they are particularly primed for dinner companionship, giving you great options with an afternoon pick up. If you're with him when dinner time arrives, going home to a prior invitation is a natural excuse, but when no excuse is wanted, you can coast on into the evening together, picking up the night mood and its special fun.

Forget the idea that nighttime is the best time to pick up a man. Make the clock your ally and approach that attractive man at a time when what's in his mind will click with what's in yours.

Following are ten proven methods for meeting men in the morning, ten for men in the afternoon and a few alternatives to singles bars for your evenings. All these approaches include opening words and are marked for the personality type most comfortable in the situation. There are many, many more places and ways to meet men. Let these suggestions be the guide that opens your eyes to the possibilities all around you.

THE MORNING MAN

It's a curious fact that male sex hormone levels are highest first thing in the morning. While our female bodies manufacture hormones around the clock, rising and falling with the month, male bodies make their hormones only during sleep. Men awaken with a high sexual awareness, but they seldom vent it, because custom prefers the nighttime for romance. Men save their desire for the evening, turning their morning urges into the energy for work and an extra awareness of the women around them. Let that awareness make you memorable.

While he's going along to work, smile at him, talk to him, and those little chemicals in his blood will send the message to his brain that here is something interesting. He responds physically as well as mentally, but still blocks the notion of intimacy. He'll never quite know why he enjoyed your pick up so much.

TEN GREAT MORNING MEETINGS

Breakfast in the diner. Women will eat lunch or dinner in a diner but almost never breakfast. If you go there between 7 and 11 A.M., you'll be surprised by the number and variety of men eating alone, and you'll notice that they look at you, since they're not used to seeing a woman at that hour. Those looks can make you feel shy, which is, surprisingly, why I recommend this approach for passive women. You just have to be yourself.

Come in and survey the room; don't run for the first booth. If no one interests you, you'll find the best table by scanning the room. If, however, you see a man you'd like to meet, a man by himself, you've probably caught his attention by making yourself visible. Take a moment to psych up, then walk over to his table with all your shyness hanging out. Say, "Excuse me, I hate eating alone. Would you mind if I shared your table so I can relax while I eat?" Speak softly and smile. Your shyness makes this work. He'll see the other men looking, understand your discomfort and feel complimented to have been chosen. You've told him he looks like a nice person, a person who can put you at ease, and more than likely he will now endeavor to show that you made a good choice. (Passive)

Walking your dog or walking where dogs are walked. Great opportunities can occur even before breakfast, especially if you live near a park where men walk their dogs. An unusual dog will draw men to you, and having a dog gives you every reason to strike up comparison conversations with dog-owning men. "Is that a Great Pyrenees?" you can ask. Whether or not the dog is what you think it is doesn't really matter as long as you praise its looks and spirit and keep your enthusiasm up. Ask the owner where he got it, how old it is, anything you can think of. A dog is a friend as well as a possession, and you flatter a man in many ways when you appreciate his pet.

If your dogs are compatible (an ill-tempered dog helps no pick up), ask your man if he'd like company on his next walk. Arrange it and be on your way—leaving him the rest of the day to think about you. (Active)

Running. Many men now start the day by running or jogging. While women are preparing to look good for an office full of other women, fit, attractive men are taking to the parks, sidewalks and countryside. Get up a little earlier, put on your makeup and jogging shorts (wear insulated tights under your shorts if it's cool) and try running with the men. Jog up beside them and smile as you pass. If an interesting man pulls ahead of you, make it a race. Run ahead, fall back. Keep it light and playful. If he's responding, offer a point to aim for, like "Race you to the water tower?" Pick a guy who looks like he won't have a coronary doing it, unless you took a CPR course. The value of racing is that when you reach your goal, you'll both be tired and can stop to rest, a comfortable time to find out who he is, where he lives and if he'd like a running partner tomorrow morning. (Active)

If you run on the same route every day, you notice other regulars. After passing them a few times, start smiling and calling "Hello" when you see them. After a few days of this, it's perfectly natural to call out, "What's your name?" to a man who interests you. If he stops, say something like, "I've been saying 'Hi' and I feel funny not knowing what your name is." Even if he just calls out his name and keeps running, you've made contact, an acquaintance-ship, and over the next days you can build on it, calling out, "Nice day" or "New jacket?" when you see he has one. Soon you'll be running together, enjoying easy, comfortable conversation. (Passive)

Catch up on the news. It's funny that so few women buy morning newspapers. Newsstands and cigar stores are packed with men in the morning, getting reading material for the commute or to mull with morning coffee. When you pick up your paper, pause to scan the front page. There's always something to comment on and it's not so hard to say to the good-looking man in the three-piecer beside you, "Can you believe what happened in El Salvador?" How can he not look and give you his opinion? Everyone has an opinion on politics, crime and welfare. When you simply point, shake your head and say, "Can you believe it?" he's free to voice any view, take any stand, since you've actually taken none. A very good way to find out what a man believes and to get all the men in the store to tell you what they believe too. Ask the most intriguing man what he thinks about another volatile subject. When he's finished with that one, the logical response from you is, "I'd like to talk more. Here's my card," or "How about lunch tomorrow?" There's no greater flattery than being asked for your opinion. A teenage boy nearly picked me up in the street a few years ago with a similar approach. He said, "Have you seen this?" and held up a news magazine, open to an interesting story. He read a paragraph and expressed amazement. We were deep in a lively discussion when a young girl came up and pulled him away with her. (Active)

Laundromats. Saturday and Sunday mornings you'll find single men in just about any laundromat. They've worked all week, and with no one to do the wash at home, this is the only time available. It's not a bad time for you, either, if you have no washing machine. And lots of men can use help with their laundry. They weren't forced to do it at home, the way most girls are, so they tend to approach their washing from a simplistic angle: Anything that doesn't go to the dry cleaners goes together in a washing machine, a powdered product goes in with it, a few quarters are inserted, and in half an hour, you get clean, wet clothes to stick in a dryer. It works fairly well, give or take a few once-white items.

Catch that guy loading all the red flannel shirts and white briefs into the machine and say, "Can I save you from pink underwear?" Yes, he'll be taken aback. Laugh and explain that the red shirts will run. He may be a little embarrassed that you were looking at his underwear, but if you tell him your load of whites could take a few more items and offer to put his shorts in with yours, you've established yourself as a nice, helpful, albeit offbeat woman. Just don't do all his wash for him; he may mistake you for his mother. A plus to sharing a washing machine is that it ties you together, allowing time to talk while you wait. In a crowded laundry, offer to share your washer or dryer right up front if your load is small. Favors always make a good start. (Active)

Ask if that man waiting has anything to read, since "There's nothing worse than waiting for laundry." Pointing it out makes him consider that talking to you is the best thing to do. Another option: When you see him struggling to fold ungainly sheets or blankets, get up and catch the loose ends. Smile and help him fold the first and hold out your hands for the second. When you're finished you might ask, "Can you help with mine?" It'll be hard to refuse. (Passive)

Bank job. Do your banking on a nonpayroll day. Successful men go to the bank a lot, but they tend to avoid Fridays when people are cashing paychecks and the lines are long. Do your paperwork in the bank, at those long tables, and casually ask that man next to you if he knows anything about these six-month certificates. This gives you a chance to air views on savings, leading into what business he's in, where he goes for lunch, etc. Most people in banks are on leave from the office and are glad to linger. (Active)

Discusing the slowness of tellers is an easy opener

on paycheck day. Once you start a conversation, the length and slowness of the line will keep it going. As you wait together each week, friendship has time to develop, until one day you can say, "We have to stop meeting this way." Suggest lunch. (Passive)

On the bus. If you take buses or trains to work, you're bound to see men waiting or riding whom you'd like to meet. One of the easiest ways to pick up a man on the bus is to look at what he's reading. There will always be a headline or photo that piques your interest if he's reading a paper or magazine, and if it's a book, look at the title and work up your curiosity. Wait until something really strikes your interest, then lean forward or tap his arm and say, "Excuse me, what's that about a garbage strike?" or "Princess Diana is really pregnant?" or "Is that Vonnegut's new book? He comes up with so many." Keep your voice warm and look him in the eye. In a sense you're interrupting him, so your friendliest smile is needed to make the difference between annoying him and making his day. Even though you're breaking into his concentration, he's more than likely just reading to pass the time, and if you show him a more appealing way to fill that time, he'll gladly put the book or paper away. As you discuss the news, ask if he takes that bus or train every day and, if he does, suggest you'll save a seat for him next time. Your interest is established and you can develop the friendship at a pace comfortable to you. (Passive)

The assertive version of meeting a man with a book or paper is the same as above, except you also ask at what stop he gets off. Which leads to, "Do you work in that neighborhood?" and "Where's a good place to eat around there? I may be in the area around lunch time this week." The logical conclusion, of course, is arranging to eat together. (Active)

Cabbing. Urban women can always win hearts by asking men to share their cab. When it's rush hour and there are four cabs to every twenty passengers and the cabbie chooses you over that man who looks like Todd Rundgren, call out to him and ask where he's headed. Any resentment he felt over the cabbie's choice vanishes quickly when he has the chance for a ride, a reduced fare and a woman's company. If he's not quite going the same way you are, a detour could be worth it. In fact, let him know it's a bit out of your way and that you think he's worth it, just don't go so far as to pay the whole fare. Then he thinks you're too eager. Conversation comes very easily when you're trapped in traffic in a cozy backseat. (Active)

Parking lots. I never encourage picking up people you work with, since facing an ex-office fling every day can make your life miserable. Still, there are many places near your work place where you'll see men you want to meet. A large parking lot used by people in many surrounding businesses will be full of men in the morning. They're safer to approach than the average man on the street because you know they have regular jobs, denoting some responsibility, and they're on the way to those jobs, so they're unlikely to carry you off. The best approach is to question him about his car. "Do you get good mileage in that Mercedes/Volvo/Oldsmobile?" followed by a compliment, "It's a beautiful car." Since questions and compliments are two favorite approaches to men, you've given him a good basis for conversation. Our hackneyed, "Work around here? Where do you eat lunch?" is a good way to shift from the car to him. If you've no time to arrange for lunch, you can always just show up at his restaurant around one o'clock. It's a small likelihood that he won't invite you to eat with him, since your encounter is still fresh in his mind. (Active)

You'll find it easy to stand and admire an expensive or classy car while the owner is parking and locking up. When he turns and sees you looking, smile, project your interest by meeting his eyes and say, "Nice car." Keep smiling and looking at him and the car. He'll pick up the conversation, but you're the one who'll have to say, "I have to go to work. Where do you eat lunch?" And then show up at his restaurant on your break. Be brave; lunch is easy. (Passive)

Elevators. You're cutting it tight in the elevators at work, because most likely that great-looking hunk works at your company. But if the building's big or he's not in your part of the office every day, it's worth a try. The closeness of elevators combined with the nervousness that many people feel about riding in them makes for a natural pick-up spot. In crowded elevators give that man a worried look and say, "Either my pocket's being picked or someone here likes me." You prove you have a sense of humor and help dispel the discomfort everyone is feeling. Any funny, upbeat coment shows him you're a woman he wouldn't mind being trapped in an elevator with, and you can follow this by asking what floor he works on, leading to "Lucky, I have to take this all the way to the fifteenth—Automated Digital" (or wherever you work). If his floor is higher than yours, say, "Too bad, you should come work at Automated Digital." And of course, when you say where you work, he says where he works, and you say, "When do you break for lunch?"

When pressed against him in the elevator, a very gutsy woman can joke, "This feels kind of good," with a laugh. It's suggestive, but your laugh shows it's partly in jest, even if your direct eye contact tells him it's not all a joke. Tell him you'd like to know his name if you're going to be this close. Since this is a seductive opening, expect him to respond in kind. (Active)

Smile at that man, get up your courage and say, "I hate elevators—well, usually," and allow yourself to look embarrassed, trying to keep your eyes on his. He'll know that your blush is a compliment; follow it with a spoken one. "Nice jacket," or something else simple is enough. Ask if he's seen a current movie.

There's a good chance he'll put the three comments together and you'll be off to the theater. (Passive)

As you see, all these common morning encounters can lead naturally to uncomplicated lunches. Use your lunch together to find out if his mind is as interesting as his looks. Since you seldom have a chance for long conversation with a man you pick up in the morning, this second casual meeting is when you'll really find out what he is like and how much more of each other you'll want to see. Bon appetit!

THE AFTERNOON MAN

At about five in the afternoon humans hit a low in their biorhythms. By three o'clock they're already starting the descent, and it's not until seven at night that they climb back out. For most families, dinner occupies that valley; it's a nice quiet time to hash over the day or catch a post-dinner snooze.

For singles it's a different world. Work ends and there's empty time before evening socializing or those favorite TV shows. A single man is not as eager to go home. Dinner alone or with a roommate is not such an exciting thought, and most restaurants don't serve until six or seven. Singles often drift through this transitional time, taking care of chores, shopping, pulling the loose ends of their lives together or winding down with a Happy Hour drink. Most important, this unstructured time is less cluttered by expectation than any other part of the day. There are many hours before bed, and singles can be inspired with a sense of infinite possibility, and openness to new experience. At five in the afternoon there's no set game plan. If your approach is right, you can make the rules as you go along.

For ten good places to start an afternoon adventure, read on.

Business district bars. Consider the businessman's bar. Although bars are less than perfect places to pick up men, those in the city's business center are terrific after-work meccas for those with no reason to rush home. Though many of the executives will be married, these two-drinks-and-off-to-the-suburbs guys are easily spotted. These places are good pickup spots because you'll seldom find rough comments or a boys-in-the-beer-hall atmosphere. The guys aren't out to score, they're just unwinding from a day of work. They'll assume you're somebody's secretary or business partner and treat you with respect, while flattering you outrageously.

Picking up a man in these bars is so easy you don't need special words. "Hey, how're you doing?" is enough to start things off, since everybody's an acquaintance. When you've started a conversation and decided you'd like to know the man better, there's nothing simpler than asking him to join you at a table. Say that you're going to eat dinner. You don't have to formally ask him to eat with you, just say you're hungry and would like to continue your conversation in a quieter setting than the bar. Now you'll know if he's married. The married man has to decline or phone or squirm. A single man will be delighted, since he has to eat anyway, and he's already enjoying your company. Be prepared to go Dutch, keeping it easy, natural and letting you decide whether you go home with—or without—him. (Active)

Pet stores. Singles kill time between day and night in different ways. Frivolous shopping is one, wandering through offbeat stores with no plan to buy, and pet stores are one of the best examples. Animal lovers tend to be nice people with an abundance of affection. Sometimes a little shy, often eccentric enough to be intriguing, the men who window-shop pet stores can be fascinating. As is often true, the best approach is a question. "Is a ten-gallon aquarium too small for cichlids?" you might ask the man staring into fish tanks. (Cichlids are a kind of fish. Pick one you recognize or read their names off the tank.) If this man owns fish, he will love to share his knowledge; if he's just looking, you can switch to admiring the exotic breeds with him. If he's examining parrots you might say, "Why do you think the prices are so high now?" If he has birds he can tell you and enjoy doing it. If not, anyone can discuss the economy. What if it's puppies or kittens? Ask, "Do dry noses really mean anything?" These are all simple questions that give him a chance to talk until he feels comfortable enough to move to a more personal subject. A good general question to ask is what animals he keeps. Then if he describes an interesting pet, you have an easy opening to say, "I'd love to see that. Mind if I drop by some time?" And when you go over, make it late afternoon, and ask if he'd like to get some dinner. (Passive)

Gourmet stores. Cheese stores that set out plates of samples, and all big specialty food stores, attract single men. You'll find intriguing foreigners stalking the aisles and all the more creative professions represented. No one shops quickly in a gourmet food store: men linger and browse for half an hour or more, considering odd labels, tasting unusual delicacies. In the stores offering samples, a party atmosphere prevails, making it easy for anyone to say to the stranger on the right, "Have you tried the Havarti?" Or, "What's that cheese you just tasted like?" After a few verbal comparisons, glide right into, "Let's see what *that* one's like." Suddenly you're paired.

In any food store, asking if he knows a good way to serve something that he's buying—a cheese, a strange mix or pasta, flatters his knowledge and can lead to involved discussion. It's natural then to tell him you'd love to taste what he's just described and offer to swap dinners sometime. Forward, yes, but food breaks many barriers.

On the other hand, if he admits he doesn't know his kasha from a hole in the ground, make some suggestions and offer to give him a demonstration at your house. Don't make it a party; a casual meal will give you a better chance to get to know him. (Active/Passive)

Office supply stores. These are great places during work hours. No one is thinking of a pick up and the men are invariably alone and wasting time. Give them an excuse to linger. When you see an interesting man, take a few moments to survey him. Look for his expensive briefcase, his Italian shoes, his silk shirt or well-tailored jacket. Then wander up beside him, smile warmly and say, "Nice briefcase. Not many executives buy their own paper clips." Maybe he's only a junior accountant, but assuming he has a good job from the way he's dressed will never insult him. This is a time when a surprise opening will work too, since he's probably bored and ready for an amusing interlude. You give him a sympathetic smile and say, "I'd sure rather be in Aspen. How about you?" You can make both your days brighter, even if he's never seen Aspen, by reminiscing about the excitement of skiing.

This is also a good place to give him one of those business cards mentioned in Chapter 7, The Basics of Approach. It's a business store, so ask him his business and hand him your card. He may have a favorite businessman's bar where you could meet later. (Active)

Lunch alone. Remember the breakfast in the diner approach? You've also got to eat lunch, and just because you go to a restaurant alone doesn't mean you have to eat by yourself. Try one of those spots with the tables for two all linked together. You're shoulder to shoulder with strangers anyway, so when you see a handsome man carrying his tray and searching for a suitable place to rest it, smile at him. Catch his eye if you can or just speak up and say, "Why don't you sit here? I hate to eat alone." Your contact can be as brief as the hour you have for lunch or can stretch into many more lunches together. (Passive)

A woman I work with told this story of picking up a lunch companion at the airport, a bold approach that could work in a restaurant as well.

She was lounging around, waiting to board a flight that wasn't scheduled to leave for several hours, and as often happens when people have ample time on their hands, her thoughts turned to romance. She spotted a man who looked as bored as she, and though he was no Robert Redford, he appeared intelligent and interesting. She followed him across the terminal at a respectable distance, and when he stopped in front of the poster-sized menu at the entrance to the airport restaurant, inspiration hit. She walked up beside him, scanned the menu quickly, then turned and announced, "I know they've got a terrific chef's salad here, but it's much too big for one person. If you promise to tell me your life story, I'll split it with you." According to her, the results were very, very spicy. (Active)

And with lunch over it's back to the stores. Where

would a nice quiet woman who loves a good book and a roaring fire find a man who's equally intelligent, sensitive and gentle? Very possibly at your local bookstore.

What's nice about meeting a man in a bookstore is that you'll rarely find manic loonies or lechers there. In fact, you may find the men shyer than yourself, but all that means is you have to be a little friendlier to help them open up.

A common sight in a big bookstore is a shaggy "man of letters" in jeans or corduroys perusing an esoteric title—something like *The Migration Habits of the Horn-billed Nutnipper*. You walk over, smile, peek at the cover of his tome and say softly, "Hmm, a gentleman *and* a scholar?"

He's not most women's idea of what a gentleman looks like, so he's amused. You keep grinning and ask if that subject is his life's work or his hobby. He may be shy, but a well-read man knows how to use words and with these couple of openers you should be able to lead him into a lively exchange—better continued over coffee at that shop down the street. (Passive)

Record stores. Hardware stores, sporting-goods stores, camera and stereo stores are all good places to be outnumbered by men, but one of the best for a pick-up is the record store. Think of a Friday afternoon. Everyone's been paid, and the first place many young men head is down to get some new tunes. The store is packed with them, and the sound level of the stereo system is cranked up so high they're all dancing in place while they sort through the bins. Sidle on up to that cute guy and say, "Want to dance?" He'll look at his own feet and, chances are, join in the joke. Ask him where he does go dancing, since he seems to do it so well. Easy to see how this can lead to a fun night out. (Active)

Back on the bus. Could meeting a man on the bus in the afternoon be any different from meeting him on the bus in the morning? Sure. For one thing, when he's going home you could get off at his stop or your stop and go for a drink together. And your approach should be different than in the morning. A man is tired after a day of work. Perhaps the bus is crowded and he's standing, limply anchored to his strap, and you have a seat. If he's near you, reach out and touch his sleeve, just a gentle tap. When he focuses on you, tell him he looks tired and you'd like to give him your seat. He'll decline. Stand up and say, "Please take it. I've been sitting all day and would love to stretch my legs. Men do it for me, let me return the favor once." Whether he sits or stands, you're already talking and can ask what he does to get so tired. Say a cool drink sometimes helps revive you and you're ready to get off together. (Active/Passive)

Look alikes. I've never favored or encouraged picking up men in the street. You have to work harder to get his attention, and his first impression can so easily be that you are one of *those* women who solicit men. But occasionally you'll spot a really great man who you know you'll never see again if you don't do something immediately. One of these irresistible types is a man who looks like a famous person. The resemblance arrests your attention, you want to move, so what do you do? The most natural thing, which is also the safest. Walk up to him and say, "You know, you look just like Steve Martin. You're not really Steve Martin, are you?" That's straight, easy and nonsuggestive. Meanwhile, he's stopped and you're talking. Now you just have to keep him going. Asking if he's told of the resemblance often is a start, and telling him he's actually younger looking, taller or more handsome than the celebrity he resembles is even better. Definitely an active move. (Active)

Standout. The other kind of man you can be hopelessly drawn to on the street is the man with one standout feature. It may be piercing eyes or thick, luxurious hair, or great shoulders. As long as it's not a directly sexual body part ("great butt" goes too far), you can zero in on that feature and say to him simply, "Great hair." It sounds spontaneous, it sounds real and it sounds like you only said it because you couldn't help yourself. If he looks embarrassed, apologize for putting him on the spot and ask where he gets his hair cut like that. The flattery sinks in and now he'll be able to start responding. (Active)

And there you have ten proven ways to find love

in the afternoon. It's an uncommon treat that you can make happen if you'll just psych up, be bold and give the men you want a chance to be part of your life.

THE NIGHTTIME

Night—the hours of love, romance and dancing in the moonlight. The time in all those wonderful old movies when the big kiss took place on the terrace, inspired by the beauty of the stars and their soft reflected glow in the leading lady's upturned eyes. There is something magically seductive about the darkness, the mystery of things concealed, features softened, eyes sparkling more brightly. And there's the pleasure of the day's responsibilities completed, you know you can let your hair down and not have to gather it up again.

I love bars and parties and the festive moods of night people, and when I was single I liked the sexy undercurrent that accompanied night games. I'm sure you do too. Even if you're shy, you enjoy the promised passion of nightlife.

Understandably that passion will affect your nighttime pick-ups. It is the time when men think most of intimacy, when their own hopes for the evening color their desires. I've devoted a separate chapter called Special Moments to the nights when you go out looking for adventure yourself. In these pages we'll concentrate on pick-ups that allow you to maintain all your options. It may be hard to go into a singles bar and pull this off, but there are many other night places where men have no firm expectations. Save the singles bar for the flings. Here are some places where you can meet men who will not be thinking mostly of bed.

Shopping malls. I know it sounds funny, but those sprawling suburban shopping malls, the kind that are closed in and climate controlled, are great places to meet men in the evening. It's not uncommon for a mall to stay open until ten or twelve at night and there will be single men there right up until the end. It's a casual atmosphere especially attractive to a shy man. In the mall he can shop, he can eat in a coffee shop or good restaurant and drink in a bar or go to a movie. But what many shy men go there for is to meet women. You'll see him strolling by himself, looking in the stores, but with little purpose. He's hoping to run into a friendly woman, but the same shyness that keeps him from scouting in a singles bar will keep him from approaching you. Walk up and ask him if he knows a place to get a pizza in the mall. Then ask if he can show you how to get there and, while he's walking with you, see if he wouldn't like to help you eat it for his trouble. Nice and easy. (Passive)

Fast food. Ever get hunger pangs around ten o'clock at night? You could go in the kitchen and whip up a bologna and cheese on white, one of my favorites, or you could freshen your makeup and go out to the nicest fast-food restaurant in the best part of your town. Most women will take the first alternative, which is why you're better off with the second. It's the one men take. A fast-food restaurant is full of kids and couples during the day, but at night there are more single men, guys who got hungry and thought it'd be nice to see some other faces while they ate. He is in the restaurant as much for company as he is for food, and he's very receptive to your interest. If he's seated, just walk up with your tray and say, "Mind if I sit here?" You can always back it with your "hate to eat alone" excuse, but it's unnecessary. You're giving him what he came out to find, so enjoy your snack and conversation and decide while you eat if it's back home or out for mutual fun afterward. (Active)

Gallery openings. Art galleries have openings, a party to introduce a new show, about once a month. You can find the notices in your daily or Sunday paper. There are few places that attract as many educated, intelligent and unusual men as an opening, and while there will be many women, most will be older and many married, so that the competition is not as great as it might appear. Dress beautifully, not in fussy clothes, but in something that defines and flatters your best points. While everyone looks at the art, you'll find most of the conversation in the crush around the wine and cheese. Squeeze in next to the man with the lively eyes and smile as you strain to reach the crackers. "Maybe if we pushed together . . ." you can say with a laugh. Stay next to him until he breaks away from the table and continue, "We got through the important part. Now, do you know anything about the show?" Walk along beside him and let the conversation come naturally as you look at the art and the other patrons (sometimes more interesting than the work). If you don't click with the first man, go back for a second glass of wine. (Active)

Concerts. Some concerts draw almost as many men wanting to meet women as they do music lovers. While classical music is for couples, rock and jazz bring out the singles, young men vibrating with energy and enthusiasm. Try for a smaller concert with unassigned seating, and arrive early. You'll find a line or crowd of fans gathering, hoping to get the best seats, and while waiting can be boring, it can also be a great opportunity to meet the people you want. Ask the man you're interested in if he thinks the artist will be on time, an easy one to answer if you've ever been to a concert. In some circles, asking for a hit of what he's smoking is also a good entrée and offering him a hit of yours is even better. Bringing food or drink for the long wait will make the man you like glad you came; when he looks at your sack of cashews, just say, "Would you like some?" and hold out the bag. In a situation potentially tedious, any approach can be golden, and when the line starts to move, just go on in and sit with the man you've been talking to. (Passive/Active)

Entertainment bars. Even better than a concert for meeting men is a bar/restaurant that books name entertainment. Though there are tables and bar seating, you're free to circulate, giving you a chance to watch the men and eavesdrop on conversations. Get your drink and wander around a while before the show begins. Listen to what the groups and couples are saying about the performer(s), pick up the gossip, all the bits that others have read or heard about, how the lead singer fell off the stage at the performance in Dayton the night before, how they expect a new song to be debuted tonight. Then when you see a man who interests you standing alone at the bar, you can slide in beside him with a wealth of conversational material. If you can't catch his eye, just open your mouth and say, "I hear that _____," and tell him the juiciest scandal you gleaned in your listening. We all love to hear gossip, especially about a famous person we're about to see perform. Chances are the man next to you will turn and ask for more. Share a couple of your gems and let him tell you what he's heard. Then you can relax and comfortably start on your own material (asking his name is a simple beginning). (Passive)

Dance clubs. Once called discos, they are now more often labeled the rock-and-roll dance bar, the New Wave dance club or the new country honky-tonk. The music may be live or recorded, but the reason to be there is the same for all: dancing your feet off. Here's the place to take your girl friend, as nearly no one goes out dancing alone. There'll be single men, but more likely in twos. Don't worry—dancing is one of the few really easy ways to split up a duet, and you start by getting out on the floor. Dance with your girl friend and really put your energy into it. The dateless man will usually be watching the dancers and will zero in on you if he sees you out their really shaking it up. Never feel embarrassed to dance with abandon, it's just what the guys watching wish they could do, and they're awed by any woman who really enjoys her body.

When you come off the dance floor, the exercise will have you psyched, and *watching* you will have the men psyched. While you're still gasping from exertion, and your girl friend has gone after her own interests, go up to the man you like, take his hand and say, "Come on, how about the next one?" or any simple invitation to dance. He's watched and he's ready, so no persuasion is necessary with this approach. Even if he says he doesn't dance, you can say with all sincerity, "How about a drink then, I'm a little overheated." Your heat will get to him. (Active)

Parties. I've always found parties the hardest social situation to handle. Somehow a room full of people who know each other just a little is worse than strangers. As cliques form, it's very easy to feel that you are the only one who isn't part of the gang, forgetting that those greeting old friends so loudly may be as nervous as you about meeting new people. On top of that there's also lots of subtle competition. Most people choose friends close to their own level of looks, so partiers will dress more carefully and work harder to stand out from the crowd, sometimes by snubbing same-sex guests trying to join the crowd. It can all add up to an uncomfortable setting, but I have learned some tricks to make parties and meeting the men there easier. First, get a drink and start moving around. Listen to the conversation, especially those involving the men you find appealing. When you hear an interesting subject, listen a little more carefully to catch the essence, but don't try to join the group. Move on and keep your eye on the man. Sooner or later he'll split from his group, and you can casually intersect his path. Excuse me, but did I hear you talking about batik?" you say. "What I've never understood is how you get the wax out of the fabric." You know he knows because that's what he was trying to explain to the others. With a serious question he can talk for five minutes while you compose yourself to introduce another subject he'd enjoy discussing, easily done by saying, "That's great, what else are you an expert in?" Afterward you can explore your areas of excellence.

An even easier approach is to watch an interesting man until he heads for the food. Follow along and dig into a dip or unusual spread and turn to him saying, "Will you taste this? There's a flavor in there I just can't figure out." The two of you can taste and then go on to talking of other things.

And there's always the most simple opener of all, an honest compliment. "That's a wonderful shirt," "What an amazing beard!" or "You have a beautiful voice," when he's talking to others. Just remind yourself that no matter how intimidating a crowd of partiers is, they're all there with a firm commitment to fun. Men want to find ways to break the ice as much as you do, so whatever you say can work if accompanied with a smile, a laugh or a warm direct gaze. (Active/Passive)

I've not suggested how to end your nighttime conversations, because that should be up to you and the man you've chosen. The romance of evening can never be planned or predicted. What starts as a simple discussion of the music can become anything when the sparks catch. But remember that decisions must be mutual. It's thrilling to be swept off your feet, but only when you've approved the sweeper.

11

Go to School

What if there was a place you could go in the evening where the men were bright, aware and interested in a good mind? What if it was also a place where those men were looking for new friendships and where, in many cases, there were many more of these men than there were women? Think you'd like to go?

Well, these places exist in every community. They're called schools, and in every town, night schools and adult extension programs are being added and refined. Some schools even have special weekend workshops where you can take two or three days of lessons and sleep over in dorms. Sometimes coed dorms.

School for an adult is nothing like when you were a kid. School is your job when you're young, it's the basis of youthful society and so it's where your position in society is decided. Whatever group you were put in as a child won't matter now. Egghead is equal to star athlete and a former whipping boy can be king in adult classes. Except for the serious long-term accredited courses, night school is like an adventure, a spirited conversation, a chance to expand your mind and social contacts.

Listen to Student X:

"I hated high school. I was so unpopular I ate lunch in the girls' room. The prom? I left school before it could even come up, but, after a few years of working as a lab assistant, I decided I might want a college degree, so I steeled myself and signed up for night courses at the local junior college. It was one of the best surprises of my life! I entered the classroom ready to slither into a seat at the back, only to be blocked by two men who laughingly insisted that I sit between them up front. After class the three of us went out for sandwiches. At the next class I went to sit with my new friends, and a man at the back said, "You going to stick with those guys the whole course?" It seemed there were many more men than women in night high school, and I found myself awash in the kind of social life I'd previously missed. I ended up dating a guy who hadn't been one of the ones vying for my attention. My confidence had been so improved, I was able to ask him for a lift home, and then in for a cup of coffee."

I admit that Student X was me, and I learned a lot that semester, including the fact that your approach to fellow students can be as important as the classes you take. To begin with, you have to find, as I did by accident, a course where there will be an abundance of male students.

Start by getting all the course catalogs for the schools in your area offering evening classes and weekend workshops. Look for the classes that interest you (never take a class you'll hate just to meet someone) and then for classes in the same school that would attract men. Anything aggressively physical is a good bet, like woodworking, carpentry, welding, engineering and auto mechanics. Then think of classes male dominated by tradition: mechanical drawing, blueprint reading, filmmaking, photography, accounting. If these subjects don't intrigue you, just make sure some of these courses are offered at the same time as the ones you want. You're assured there'll be enough men around the school during the hours you are there.

Find out what rooms the male-dominated courses are in and walk by when one of these classes is letting out. See an attractive man exiting? Step toward him and smile. Gently block his path, look him in the eyes and say, "Excuse me. How is that class? It sounded interesting in the brochure." If he responds well, you back it up with, "Do you have a few minutes? Let's get some coffee and I'll pick your brain a little more." And you never have to get near a welding torch. (Active)

Here's another way to meet men in a class you don't want to take. Check your catalog's fine print.

Many schools let you drop a course after the first class if you're dissatisfied. If your school allows this, sign up for something you could use but are not sure that you will enjoy. On your first night, look at your classmates, and when you get a chance, smile at the men or join in discussion. If no man interests you and you decide you won't enjoy the class itself, go to your second-choice class and sign up late. If you like a man and not the course, drop it and walk by the class for two days while it's letting out. Say hello and walk on. By the third night ask the man how it's going, if he isn't already talking to you. Since you're now on speaking terms, it won't be hard to start a conversation. (Passive)

Another way to meet other students outside your own classes is to spend an hour or two in the registration area on sign-up day. There are always huge crowds. Just mill about and try looking a man in the eye and giving him a sympathetic smile. In that madhouse he may see you as an oasis of calm and launch into a conversation. This is also a wonderful time to be useful. Learn where the stations are and how to move through them, so that you can say, "Are you lost?" or "Do you need help?" to a man who looks confused by the mob scene. If the first doesn't need it, the second will be grateful for your assistance, and since part of helping is asking what course he's taking, you'll know where to find him later. Don't be afraid to tell him that you'd like to get something to eat when you're through. If he's been there a while, he'll be hungry or thirsty too. Ask if he's tried the place across the street, and you'll be on your way. (Passive)

My husband taught photography and says that this trick is used about once a semester, though usually by male students. It's a gutsy variation on dropping out after the first class. Wait until the first class of a heavily male course is fifteen minutes under way, then walk in and sit in the back. You'll have every man's attention briefly, including the attention of the teacher, who'll ask for your registration card. To this you reply, "I just signed up this minute, and they didn't have any more cards." Most teachers will tell you to be sure to bring it to the next class. You agree, sit back and see what the other students and the class is like. If you like both, you can still sign up late. If not, you've made your impression on the men in class, and you can say to any one of them, "Did I miss anything in the first minutes?" (Active)

But enough on finding where the right men may be. Here is a list of courses that you may enjoy yourself where there are sure to be many male students. They're all available in the evening or on weekends. Many even feature body contact.

Try a life saving/resuscitation course. These classes are often offered free by Y's, hospitals, police departments or Jaycees. It's a short, fun course, besides being a very good way to meet brawny firemen and ambulance attendants, a few policemen and some concerned nice-guys. The mouth-to-mouth resuscitation in unfortunately now taught on a doll, but you will learn how to pick up and carry your fellow students. The general embarrassment about touching people you don't know encourages comradery and makes it easy to pick up strangers. (Passive/Active)

If you've ever been awed by Bruce Lee, why not try a short self-defense or karate course? They are gentler than most of the other martial arts but still almost entirely male dominated. An additional plus is that knowing self-defense will give you confidence. And for every fear a woman sheds, she likes herself better and so does everyone else.

You don't have to feel unfeminine in a class full of kickers and choppers. Grace is essential to these courses, and you can excel in the dancelike movements. The etiquette of control in karate, Kung Fu and the like keeps down the rambunctious energies, so you won't find a Rocky gym scene. For all these reasons I strongly recommend martial arts for passive women. You'll banish some of those feelings of weakness while enjoying conversation-provoking physical contact. A good approach to a man you meet in this course is to invite him to a martial arts demonstration or Bruce Lee festival. Buy a couple of tickets and tell the man you like that they've fallen into your hands. No need for elaborate lying, just be vague. Let him know that you have them, he has to pay nothing, and that you'd enjoy his company.

Make it a friend's invitation, with no expectations, and he won't feel funny about being treated. Then show him the best time you know how. The next treat will be his. (Passive)

Have you ever found yourself stranded on a dark road at 2 A.M. because your car malfunctioned? Many women have. It's one of the most helpless feelings I know, and if it's happened to you, basic car care may be a course you can't pass up. It's meant for nonmechanics, but most women shy from it because it's dirty. It also breaks fingernails, but the classes are full of men.

The more basic the course, the greater the variety of men there will be. Many will be people like you, car owners with no interest in mechanics as a profession. And the less a man knows about cars, the easier it will be for you to strike up a conversation. All men are supposed to be auto experts, so when they don't know, they're likely to look for another convenient way to express their masculinity. Like flirting with a female student. If you ask one of them to help you—not to explain, which he may not be able to do, but physically help you, you'll charge his ego and make your own work easier. (Passive)

The other way to make a lasting impression in this class is by being willing to get dirty. Wear old clothes that fit well and accent your curves without limiting your movements. Then actively participate. You don't have to be the first, but volunteer to get down and look under the car. Don't pretend to be an expert, but do show you're serious about being there. Men are really more comfortable treating you as an equal. If anyone snickers at the way you turn your first bolt, just grin at him and take it as a friendly ribbing. Remember that men hurl playful insults at each other all the time. A great move is to bring some beautiful clothing along and change after class while everyone is still milling around. Go all out with a clinging or swirling skirt and high heels. The contrast will knock them out, and it's then that you say to the man you've been admiring, "Do you have a *working* car? I could sure use a lift." He'll be intrigued enough that a no is unlikely. (Active)

If you are interested in specific kinds of men, consider the special classes that might attract them. If you live near a lake or on a large river or sound, there should be a sailing school near you. You don't need to own a boat yourself. You will meet men in school who have them, men who probably have more money that you do to spend on all manner of fun times. Look in your Yellow Pages for sailing school. Since you'll be on the water, you'll want to dress appropriately. Find out too how lunch is handled. You may have to bring your own food, meaning that you can pack an oversized bag of fried chicken, apples, cookies, all things that can be easily shared and easily offered to the man you've begun to admire. (Active)

If you're really brave and near the ocean or sound, consider the most bonding of courses; scuba diving.

Like sailing there is no need to own your equipment until you find out if it's a sport you'll want to continue after class. And like sailing, there will be more men than women and men who are probably richer and more adventurous than the average guy on the street. Of course, it takes a strong heart and a total absence of claustrophobia to do well in this course, as raw panic will not make the impression you're after.

The great plus in diving class is the buddy system. Every time you go below you must have someone to accompany you, and that person will share the exhilaration of the new experience. It can make you and your buddy very close. It's good to start scouting for your diving partner in the earliest class. Asking the man, "Do you have any experience in this?" is an easy opening. Since you both know that you'll need someone to buddy with, you can say after a few minutes of conversation, "Do you have a partner to dive with?" If he hasn't, ask if he'd go with you. Once he says yes, shared rides home, lunches and dinners will probably follow. (Active)

There's one course that you may like to try which is an actual job preparation. If you're a teetotaler though, just skip to the next section because I'm talking about bartender's school. This course is easy and fun and there is a real demand for female barkeeps at better restaurants and resorts. Meeting men in the class will be easy and meeting men on the job afterwards even more so. (Passive)

How about those courses women say they really want to take? Most are brimming with women, making them hard places to meet men, but here are some pleasant exceptions that let you double your fun.

Filmmaking was mentioned up front. Video classes are another good choice, and both attract a lot of dynamic men. The only problem is getting between them and their cameras so they'll notice you. Standing in front of the lens is a good way.

"I'd never really looked at Sonya in class," said Tom. "I knew she was kind of cute but I was there to learn camera work, not look for girls. When we started making our own films, she was just there one day, offering herself as a character for my film if I'd be in hers. I realized I'd never really looked at her until I saw her on the editing machine. The film wasn't much, but I kept getting caught up in her face. I saw the way her face lit up all over when she smiled, I fell totally in love with her."

It wasn't quite as accidental as Tom thinks. Sonya had been thinking about him from the first class.

"His dedication was part of what attracted me to Tom. He was nice looking for sure, but he was also totally wrapped up in being a filmmaker. I tried to talk to him on two occasions and couldn't get through. I'm too shy to outright ask a man to go out with me, and Tom was too preoccupied to pick up my signals. As my last stab I worked up my courage and offered to help with his movie. I was petrified! When he was filming I kept fantasizing about the two of us on a beach at sunset, rolling in the surf, all that really romantic stuff. I looked right at him through the camera and sent those thoughts out and it worked. He says I lit up. I was trying like anything to light him up. He calls me 'Moviola' now, after the editing machine that helped me pick him up."

If quiet little Sonya did it, so can you. The budding filmmaker needs subjects, and once you're on his film you've become, in a small way, a permanent part of his life. Seduce his camera and the man will follow. (Passive)

Still-photography classes are much like filmmaking except that there will be more women in the course. But when you get that camera, you can roam all over the school taking pictures of the men you like. If you're shy you can snap and walk on, smiling if he catches you. When you get a really good photo, make him a small print and when you next see him, present it with a simple, "It came out so well I thought you might like a copy." You don't have to explain to him why you took the picture. Just tell him he's photogenic and you'd like to take some more pictures some time. Then set a time. (Passive)

Ask him to pose. "Hey, stand on that waste basket for a second! Great. One more over here. Could you jump in the air?" Get him involved and then ask if he'd do some more posed shots—at your home or somewhere away from school. There have been many famous male photographer/female model love affairs; who says you can't turn the tables? (Active)

Have you avoided life-drawing classes because you didn't want to compete with a nude model? Many women feel uncomfortable, but men find the course compelling because most models are women. A real live naked woman to look at sounds good, but when they get in the class few ever try to date her. The model can approach the men easily, but usually doesn't, so while the men are prepared to be titillated, let them turn their interest to you. Comparing drawing approaches is simple, and if you can be the one woman in class who doesn't criticize the model, you'll stand out.

I've noticed working at *Oui* and other magazines that women are very defensive when they see men admiring nude women.

"Those boobs are too big to be real."

"They don't look that way without makeup."

"They're totally airbrushed."

"She looks like her IQ matches her chest size," and "She'd never go out with you" are the most common things I hear women saying to men about those girls who appear in magazines. They don't gain much in the men's eyes that way. Such comments are more likely to make the men search for things to compliment in the photos, to defend the models against unpleasant jealousy.

But I've also seen that rare woman smart or secure enough to say, "Oh, she is pretty, isn't she? Nice hair, and look at that velvet chair. Boy, I'd love to have one of those." This pulls the man's attention away from the photos and impresses him with the woman's confidence.

Use this approach in your life-drawing class. If he's talking about the model, join him in admiring her good points, then start discussing how hard it is to get the folds right in the drape covering her stool. Men will test you, often unconsciously, for negative impulses. He probably likes you more than her, but before he gets involved he wants to know if you're going to smother him with possessiveness. (Active)

Test him. When he's talking about the model, say you had considered applying for her job. Use the skills of observation you've been developing (see Basics of Approach) to interpret his response. Actually, if he says anything at all he's probably been observing you. In any case, he'll end up thinking about your qualifications. (Active)

If you can't put yourself on the line, you can still get his attention by asking if you could sketch his hands. Faces are hard and if your drawing is less than perfect, it's more embarrassing than flattering. Hands draw a less personal reaction. Sit near and start drawing while he works. When he catches what you're doing look him in the eyes and say, "Do you mind? Your hands are so strong/well-formed/(anything positive)." Keep glancing up and smiling as you work. (Passive)

These are only a few of the endless possibilities for picking up men in school. Investigate your town's night schools and extension courses and you'll come up with many that I've missed. School is a social as well as educational institution, and many of the men you meet there have signed up for the same reasons as you, to increase their knowledge and multiply their friendships. Make some of those friendships yours.

12

Special Men

"Where do I meet a rich old man who'll shower me with gifts?" asked my office assistant Lisa. I was typing and ignored her, but she came back a few minutes later, leaned on my typewriter and said, "I'm very serious. Why don't you write about how to meet someone like that?"

"Because the approaches I'm writing down will work with all men," I told her, "Now get your hands off my manual return."

"But how do we find them?" she continued. "How am I going to know that the man in the . . . [scanning my interrupted page] . . . newsstand . . . is rich and will be able to take me to Acapulco if this cold weather keeps up?" And thinking about it I realized she had a point.

Almost every time I spoke to a woman about this book, she asked, "Are you going to tell me *where* to meet my doctor (or jock or French diplomat)?" Because they all asked, I concentrated on the word "where" and found lots of wheres. But they almost always *also* mentioned a specific kind of man, a man who represented the ideal man to them. I began to think back on all the kinds I'd heard them ask about and several groups emerged.

These, I've decided, are the Special Men. The men who by action or reputation have earned prominent places in female fantasy. If so many women wanted them, I'd make a section exploring their personalities, preferences and stomping grounds. I started with Rich Men so Lisa could go to Acapulco as soon as possible and leave me to finish the rest. Eighteen is a difficult age.

My continuing research uncovered not only the basic groups, but a few simple truths to help the women who don't find their special man listed here. Whatever type appeals to you, you should remember the following:

1. Every man has a home, and men in the same professions and social groups tend to live in the same places.

2. Single men eat in restaurants much more often than women, and professions and social groups tend to eat in the same places.

3. All men are consumers, and every profession and social group buys things peculiar to the group. Athletes buy sports equipment, artists buy art supplies, rich men buy expensive luxury items.

4. Single men tend to spend their leisure time with other single men who have similar interests.

What does it all mean? This: Find an apartment

house across from a hospital and it will be full of doctors. Follow a famous man into a restaurant and you're likely to find other famous men inside. Go in a sporting goods store and it will be full of athletes, and when you see a cute twenty-year-old college man go into a pub, there will, more than likely, be other twenty-year-old, adorable college men on the inside, just waiting for you to come in and start a conversation.

Read on. In the next seven sections you'll find the most-often-asked-about men, and how and where to meet them. Dare to go after the man of your dreams. If he isn't included, consult the list above, look around your community and find out where men of his type congregate.

And if you find a spare Rich Older Man, send him to Lisa. Her suitcases are packed and cluttering up my office.

RICH MEN

Rich men come in three basic varieties: older and financially secure; young to middle-aged and on the way up; and the very wealthy heirs to great fortunes who are rich from cradle to grave.

I know women—actresses, dancers and models— who make a second career out of dating rich men. It seems that wherever these women are, a rich man will magically appear to lavish them with attention and pay their bills. From these friends I've learned some facts, particularly about the older, divorced or marginally married rich man. Most of these gentlemen spent their youth working so hard that they were barely aware that they had wives and children. Suddenly, at fifty or sixty, they decide to enjoy life, only to discover their alienation from family and friends. They feel cheated. They're ready for their reward, for something frivolous, something entirely conceived for their pleasure.

Nothing fulfills this wish better than an attractive, fun-loving woman. You don't need to be young or especially beautiful to appeal to such a man. You do need to be lively, spontaneous and adept at maintaining enthusiasm. You need to know the classic ways of wasting money because he really believes that it can buy happiness. The woman who's right for him agrees, and their happiness revolves around this shared notion.

If shopping for clothes lifts your spirits, you'll appreciate a rich older man. Beautiful clothing means more to him than to most men and slightly old-fashioned dresses particularly attract him. Fitted bodices with cleavage tend to catch his eye as do high heels and sparkly jewelry (*good* fakes are fine), because they remind him of the beauty queens that he forsook in his youth. That's why he also likes coiffed hair and skillful makeup.

He doesn't see many women on the street who

match his tastes, so his quest for old-fashioned beauties will take him to the old-fashioned centers of hedonism.

He can be found in the casinos of Las Vegas or Atlantic City at the high-stakes games. He's the man with the big bank roll who's betting carefully and considering his moves. Slip in beside him and ask him to help you place a bet. A touch of helplessness will make him receptive. If he's a classic Rich Older Man, he'll enjoy the image of you beside him and feel comfortable impressing you in the way he's accustomed—through his money. (Active)

The Rich Older Man also likes to spend his money eating well. Play on his paternal instincts in the expensive, formal restaurants where he's likely to lunch. One of my favorite friends, a well-known ex-dancer, finds these distinguished gentlemen at the bar. She recognizes them by their expensive clothes and Wall Street gossip. "Could you light my cigarette, please?" is her favoriate opening. It's as phony as her scarlet nails, but this is the one time when phony has tremendous appeal. She's proclaiming frivolity, and the more helpless this very competent lady appears, the more she projects "I am a luxury item." They buy her lunch, they take her out, and they give her gifts. Under any other circumstances I'd say she was using them, but in this case she's fulfilling their fantasy, and they are very happy to treat her well in return. (Active)

Expensive, traditional men's stores, especially those

with fine tailoring departments, are also good places to meet a Rich Older Man. Compliment him on something he's wearing—his jacket, his tie—and ask him if he got it in that store. If he did, ask him to tell you, or better, take you, to the rack where he got it. Again, that slight helplessness will enhance your appeal. If the garment came from another store, smile and ask for complete step-by-step directions. The longer you keep him talking, the more comfortable he'll feel when you say, "I'll never find it. Couldn't you just go with me?" (Passive/Active)

Corny as it sounds, another place to find this man is at a yacht or country club. Many women have taken summer waitressing jobs in such spots and become close to an older member. When you serve a man several times and note that he's seldom seen with a woman, you can ask quite easily why he's alone. Smile warmly and he'll begin looking forward to your friendly talk. You can then ask what other sports or hobbies he enjoys and say in response, "I'd love to try that sometime." He'll most likely be glad to have you try it with him. (Passive)

If you find acting helpless and dressing up unappealing, remember that these men are not for every woman. Don't push yourself to be what you're not. Women like my friend the dancer naturally love these men in the way they need to be loved. But if that's not you, try the more wary but modern Man on the Way Up.

The biggest problem with Men on the Way Up

is that they are usually married. I don't recommend attacking marriages, so we'll concentrate on finding the few rising stars who are single or divorced.

Urban apartment complexes, those self-contained cities with astronomical rents, are where most single men on the way up live. An older man may have a house in the country, but the younger men who are concentrating on piling up the fortune want to be close to their businesses. The apartment complex with its own stores and restaurants ideally fits their busy life-style. You can meet the residents shopping there. Visit the drugstore around seven o'clock at night and ask the well-dressed man who catches your eye, "Are those hair-care systems really any better than plain shampoo and conditioner?" Any similar practical question will get him talking, and you can follow up by asking about the apartments. "Are they really worth the money?" can lead to, "Do you think I could look at yours to get an idea?" When he takes you up, you'll know right away if he lives alone and whether the relationship seems worth pursuing. (Passive)

The coffee shops in these complexes are fine places to meet single residents, and the old approach of saying you hate to eat alone works on the rich as well as the poor. He'll assume right off that you're another resident and be predisposed to be neighborly. (Passive/Active)

Take-out restaurants near a complex and in all

high-rent neighborhoods are other havens for single men. Delicatessen or ethnic specialty restaurants are particularly good since rich men usually cultivate tastes beyond McDonald's or Burger King. "That Westphalian ham looks great. Have you had it?" is simple and takes you into, "What do you recommend? I'm in the mood for something unusual." That's a great leading remark when you deliver it with a sparkle in your eye. (Active)

Dress up in some nice classy clothes and go inspect the new Mercedes-Benz at your local dealership. Any man you strike up conversation with here is likely to have some money, and if he's thinking of buying, he'll love to discuss the merits of the car he wants to purchase. Maybe he'll even take you along for a test ride. Don't lie and say you're considering buying the car, just tell him you love the design and came in on impulse to take a look. He will understand your appreciating quality merchandise and with luck will see you as a kindred spirit. (Active)

Many of these hints for finding a man on the way up also apply to the sons of the wealthy. They inhabit the same apartment complexes, but they're the residents you see in the coffee shop in the middle of the day. A young man with money won't take a job that limits his freedom. He's more likely to work at home in a creative profession, as a photographer, a songwriter/singer or a painter. He's the man in the drugstore who's dressed more casually than the other patrons. Approach him as you would any man in these circumstances. (Passive)

Trendy resorts are always excellent places to find rich men's sons. Check gossip columns and talk shows to find out current favorites or simply try any elegant vacation spot in the Caribbean. None are too costly, and they do attract an exciting crowd. When you see the man who attracts you, be direct. On vacation you can get by telling a man that you'd love to have dinner with him. If he takes it wrong, none of your friends will know. (Active)

Closer to home, ocean, beach and lake communities are stocked with the rich and near rich. Spend a weekend nearby. Jogging on the beach can put you in contact with many attractive fellow runners. (Passive)

Rich men are not unattainable. The only power they have that you don't is buying power. They don't want to be taken in by a grasping woman, but if you like a rich man first as a person, he won't mind that you like his money too.

FAMOUS MEN

A famous man can be won with many of the approaches that work on men in general. Never forget that famous men have as many problems meeting women they can be compatible with as anyone else. In fact, they often have more difficulties. Their careers leave little time to give to their relationships, and because they are so well known, they can't just go out and meet a woman on the street. The same fame that makes them desirable hurts their access to women. That's why so many famous men pair off with women in their own business. If they could comfortably meet you, chances are they'd enjoy your company just as much as that fellow famous person's.

Famous men tend to congregate in the big cities like New York, Los Angeles and Washington. If you're serious about pursuing your fame fantasy, take your vacation in one of these cities, charting beforehand who will be there, where he'll be staying, where he'll be working and maybe even the names of some restaurants near his work and hotel. How do you find all this information? With a little simple sleuthing.

Start with *Variety*. This big show business tabloid is the voice of the entertainment industry. It's not an exact guide, and your favorite may not show up there every week, but by reading all the notices, you'll begin to learn what hotels are popular with different kinds of entertainers. You'll also find where movies are being made that require performers to take up residence in a town, perhaps one close to yours, for several weeks. Most such towns offer little entertainment for the stars after the day's shooting is done, and they welcome hints from helpful locals.

If you are really serious about meeting the famous, call information in Los Angeles or New York and ask for Celebrity Services, Inc. They put out the *Celebrity Bulletin,* a daily accounting of who is visiting one or the other of these cities. You have to subscribe, and the price is high, about forty-five dollars a month, but it tells day-by-day who has come to town, why they are there, how long they plan to stay and, quite often, what hotel they are staying in.

A cheaper, but less thorough, way to find where a famous man can be reached is to watch the promotion credits on a talk show. Almost all talk shows make an announcement some time during the presentation of where their guests stay. Has it never occurred to you that you could just call up and talk to your hero at the hotel? Most shows are taped the same day they're shown, so just wait till next morning and call the hotel around 10 A.M. (their time). You can get the number easily from information, and when you call, just ask with cool authority for his room. Chances are they'll put you right through. Afraid you'll get tongue-tied? Call with a purpose. Say you're a great fan working on a profile, which I'm sure you'd love to do. Don't lie outright. Don't say you work for a paper or are writing a book, just say you'd love to get his opinions on a couple of things: new trends in his work, the influence of New Wave, whether he would ever date a fan, how he feels about the new, more assertive woman—you get the drift. Whatever else you say, joke and praise him and keep telling yourself he's a human being, susceptible to the same emotions as any other man or woman. He'll like to hear his name, he'll like genuine well-conceived compliments, perhaps on his voice, his ability to portray emotions or the intelligence he brings to his work; and he will surely enjoy a warm, friendly, confident female voice saying all these things to him. You can ask if he has a few minutes to meet you face-to-face for a couple more questions, saying you'll come to his room or the hotel dining room. He'll probably tell you he hasn't the time, but he just might be intrigued. No matter how the conversation turns out, just speaking with a famous man you admire is a memory to cherish. (Passive)

A hotel known for its famous guests could make your vacation the trip of a lifetime. In resort towns like Las Vegas or Tahoe, the performers usually stay at the hotel they're appearing in. In New York they tend to spread around, from the Drake (where I first met Billy Carter) to the Mayflower (host to famous rebels), to the Chelsea (like the Mayflower, but with more musicians), to the Elysee (a celebrity hide-out hotel), to the sedate old Plaza (everyone, sometime) on up to the new and fantastically regal Helmsley Palace (the famous and exceptionally rich). In L.A., the Beverly Hilton shows up again and again in the *Celebrity Bulletin,* as does the Beverly Wilshire, and I personally stumbled onto a great place for musicians—the Hyatt Continental of Hollywood.

If you're at one of these hotels and see a famous man alone in a bar or restaurant, try approaching him and telling him quietly, in the warmest way possible, that you think he's wonderful. Don't squeal or otherwise draw attention to him, and don't ask for his autograph. Just act like an equal and pretend that it's the most natural thing in the world for you two to be talking. If he's there alone, there's a good chance he'll ask if you'd like to have a drink with him. (Active)

Some famous people are so accustomed to crowds that they are uncomfortable being alone. If he's aloof, don't press, but if he responds at all, hang in there and talk about him. The key is showing respect, letting him know you appreciate the honor of meeting him—and it *is* an honor to meet a famous person—without fawning. Again, act as an equal, but an admiring one.

In New York and L.A. there are huge TV network buildings where many, many shows are taped every day. People tour the sound stages hoping to see a famous face, but few consider all these buildings have restaurants where most of the personalities eat lunch. Find the buildings in the phone book and go to the restaurants between 12 and 2 in the afternoon. You can even call the network offices and ask when a show taped there breaks for lunch. This kind of information is surprisingly easy to get.

Start by sitting alone and ordering lunch. If you see a famous man you want to meet, try to find a moment when he's alone, even if he's on his way back from the men's room. Try to step in his path, hopefully right into him, saying gently, "It's a pleasure bumping into you like this," followed quickly by, "You're a fantastic actor/newscaster/singer." Then move aside, giving him a big, seductive smile. It's a very active start, but it can get strong reactions. If you see him watching you after you've returned to your table be ready to leave when he does so you can walk up to him and say, "I hope I didn't startle you, but I couldn't help letting you know how I feel about you." If he stays to talk with you, great. If he doesn't, say, "Eat here every day? Maybe I'll see you tomorrow." Next day you can smile and say "Hi." Give him the chance to see that you're not just a fame groupie, that what you really want is him. It's hard to hold out against flattery. (Active)

The main thing to remember in dealing with celebrities is that they are human. Most such men are grateful when you simply treat them as you would your less famous friends.

OLDER MEN

I'd often heard the phrase "older man" and had a pretty good image of who he was. The older man was tall and gray at the temples. He dressed in expensive suits and had a good job where he was called sir. He had an infinite store of knowledge and a long list of great restaurants up his tailored sleeve. He spoke well and favored young women whom he would take on cruises and could introduce as his niece if the need arose. He was a great guy but frankly one that never caught my interest.

Then I married a man fifteen years my senior who was exuberant and funny, who dressed as he damn well pleased, who had forty-four years of fascinating experience without being stuffy and who was only a father to his son.

I learned that older doesn't have to mean daddy. You can't place men over forty into a single mold any more than you can men under twenty. An older man can be fatherly, distinguished, exuberant, stuffy or childish or any combination. There's a lot in the way of self-knowledge and experience that an older man has to offer, as long as you enjoy him for himself.

In picking up an older man, remember to move at a slightly slower pace. He grew up in a world where the men approached the women and called every shot. He may agree in principle with the concept of liberation but still not know how to react when a woman walks up and begins a leading conversation. That doesn't mean he isn't flattered. My mail at *Oui* tells me that older men fantasize about assertive women as much as younger men. The older man is just less prepared to see his fantasy become a reality. Ask him for a match, ask him for the time, talk about the weather or how nicely the band is playing. Don't come on with too many compliments and don't offer to buy him a drink. An older man is more likely to jump to conclusions and suspect an overly friendly stranger of being a call girl.

Meeting an older man takes a little time. Better to say, "Gee, if you're going to see that Picasso show, I'd love to go along," than "Let me take you to the Picasso show at City Museum; I have tickets." Don't take all the control away from him or he's likely to feel pushed.

Classic clothing puts an older man at ease. He may love to look at cleavage and tight jeans, but if your style is too revealing or faddish, he'll feel uncomfortable introducing you to his friends, as I found out when I once dated a rather famous older man.

I met him at a formal business function where I wore a suit. We got on well so I visited him at his home the next week and we began dating. The first two evenings he took me to out-of-the-way restaurants. When I met him for the third date, he broke down in exasperation and told me I was embarrassing him by dressing like a tart. I was just dressing in the tight skirts and low cut blouses popular that spring in New York, but he was appalled.

"I'd like to introduce you to my friends," he said, "but with our age difference and the way you dress, I'm afraid they'll think I'm a fool."

It may seem narrow-minded for a man to care how you dress, but his fear of appearing the fool to his friends can't be ignored. The Older Rich Man is an exception; he likes the attention a flashy woman

149

brings, but for most older men, the less noticeably you dress, the more comfortable they'll feel.

Some older men really do have paternal instincts. If he starts out treating you as a little girl, you'll know pretty quickly if you like it. If not, try telling him, "You know you're much too young-looking to be my father."

If you enjoy being protected, let his fatherly feelings help you pick him up. In the supermarket ask him to help you add up your purchases before you check out. If he lives in your building, ask if he'll help with your leaky faucet. On the street, see if he'll help you find an address, and in a bar, tell him you'd like some company to hold the wolves at bay. It's a little old-fashioned, but so is the paternal man you're interested in.

You will find older men almost anywhere men gather. The suggestions that follow apply mostly to the distinguished older man most common in fantasy.

A dinner party will yield more older men than a cocktail mixer. Ask a friend to introduce you if you see a man down the table who looks intriguing, and put out the word, between parties, that you're available. (Passive)

Classical or jazz concerts are wonderful places to meet an older man because they give you a perfect excuse to talk. All you have to do is catch his eye at intermission to say, "Are you enjoying the concert?" smile and present yourself with confidence and he'll probably begin discussing the music. When it's time to return to your seats, you can feel free to say, "When will we see each other again?" If he's vague, suggest the next concert, saying, "Music can't really be appreciated alone." (Active)

Museums and art galleries are naturals for the older man. Society today may show less interest in culture, but an older man remembers when art had more impact. There are generally very nice restaurants near big museums and, after you've discussed the art, telling the man who catches your eye that you're hungry and plan to go to one of them will probably encourage him to ask to go along. (Passive)

It may surprise you how many older men can be found at tennis clubs. A good way to meet an athletic older man is to watch his game, wait until he comes off the court and then greet him by asking "Are you the club pro?" It's tremendously flattering to be taken as an expert, especially when he knows that you've just watched him play. He'll give you the help you want, which can easily lead to drinks at the bar. (Passive/Active)

Give the older man a try. There's so much you can learn from his experiences. Like how you'll react in a few years when you are an older woman and a man ten years your junior catches *your* eye.

YOUNGER MEN

The eighties is the era of the older women. Though they know Mrs. Robinson only from reruns, young men are fascinated by a woman who knows her mind and is unafraid to ask for what's on it. For many the idea of old-fashioned femininity is part of the turn-on, the stockings and dresses and perfume sheltering an incongruous strong will. I see the signs of this change all over.

Recently a curvy, fortyish woman came in from Texas to do some modeling. The editors gathered around this woman and started slyly inquiring as to what kind of man she liked. She glanced around the circle, squared her shoulders, thrust out her considerable chest and drawled, "All kinds, as long as they're over six foot, under thirty and well put together." The over-thirty editors slunk back to their offices, but the twenty-four-year-old, six-foot music editor took her out for a great night on the town.

When he dragged in exhausted the next day, the young editor said only, "I never had a thing for older women, but when they're that straightforward I'll take them over any twenty-year-old." A straightforward approach is the best way to meet a younger man. The dream he has about an older woman is that she'll take charge because she knows what she wants. You can even be a little suggestive with a younger man. He has a certain awe of you as his elder, especially if you dress in the good sophisticated clothing he associates with a woman who wields some power. A lady in a tailored suit and silky blouse can graze the thigh of the college man she's talking to and say, "Do you play football? Your muscles are so firm" and excite him no end while throwing him totally off balance. The clothes and the words don't quite match, leaving him intrigued by your many facets, by how much less predictable you are than the younger women he's used to.

He really does want you to be different from those younger women. You don't appeal to a younger man by looking like a parody of youth, by dressing fourteen when you're forty. Silks, cashmeres, well-fitted slacks and tailored skirts with expensive, quietly sexy blouses give you that rich professional look, that look of competence that catches his attention.

With this man you should think of the approaches described throughout this book that show you at your most competent. Don't be afraid to say to him in a bar, "May I buy you a drink?" But better is sending the drink to him at the bar or his table. It's a good chance no one has ever approached him so elegantly, making your impression strong and immediate.

I've not included many places to meet the younger man because he's found almost any place you go, and any time he's alone is a good time to introduce yourself. What follow are places to find him in particular abundance.

Any outdoor concert will attract hundreds of younger men. A simple walk through the park gives you the opportunity to ask the man on the edge of the crowd, "Who's performing? What's the event?" and progress to a frank compliment like, "God, you've got great eyes," causing a definite recession in his interest in the music. (Passive)

Record stores, stereo stores and sporting goods stores cater to young interests. If he's not there with three of his buddies, start a leading conversation. Chances are he's just waiting for some excitement to come into his life. (Active)

Check the Go to School chapter. A student can be particularly susceptible to an intellectual challenge like, "Would you like to explore the older woman/ younger man mystique?" delivered with a straight face. (Active)

Of all these suggestions, the best younger man adventures can be found in college-break towns. Here I would even recommend taking a woman friend along; there are so many men prowling for excitement that you may need her help to maintain control. Beach and ski resorts like Fort Lauderdale, Florida, Wildwood, New Jersey, Aspen, Colorado, and Lake Tahoe, California, are legendary gathering spots for college students. With a little investigation, you'll find many others close to home.

Be sure to reserve a hotel room several weeks in advance. Not only do quality accommodations go, but all rooms vanish fast as the Easter week approaches. There will be young women along with the men, but don't get caught up in competition fears. For one thing, there are always more men than women, and for another, what you offer a man is different from what a woman his own age offers. The young man who notices and responds to you does so because you project something the younger woman doesn't. He won't be wishing he had her instead.

Try the big dance clubs present in all these resort towns to meet the men. You can easily ask them to dance until you find one you really like, and then tell him, "Let's get away from the noise for a while," and lead him out for a walk on the beach, along the lake or back to your place for more intimate partying.

Younger, older, in between, there are no barriers on whom a woman can date today. When you want to walk over to that downy-cheeked young man, remember the words of our weary but still happily wiser music editor, and approach him with confidence.

ATHLETES

Five years ago athletes might not have been included in this section. So many women once derided them as brainless and one-dimensional that I was embarrassed by my voyeuristic love of them. Yet suddenly fitness is in for everyone, and while women are running, playing tennis, working out, swimming and even lifting weights, they are also casting glances at the men toiling beside them.

The simple effect of playing sports is a well-toned, beautiful body. But as many of you begin to admire the sculpted physiques of active men, you start to feel shy and awkward about your own. Just how much beauty do athletes require of the women they date? Jimmy Connors married a Playboy Playmate; Reggie Jackson is reputed to date only beautiful stewardesses. So many professional athletes grow up with small-town expectations, it's no surprise they grab for all the goodies they can gobble when they make the big time and start meeting beautiful women. That's natural human gluttony, but you don't have to be intimidated by it. Look at some of the other greats. Bjorn Borg may be the best tennis player of all time. Beautiful women vied for his attentions, and did he go for a fragile Kewpie Doll? No, he fell for a very real woman whose most outstanding attributes are her energy, drive and intelligence. Former L.A. Rams quarterback Vince Ferragamo is movie-star handsome. And his wife? A strong, athletic woman, no glittering mantelpiece trophy. And does anyone remember the great romance between Harold Connolly and his beloved Olga? Harold was a hammer thrower for the U.S. Olympic team and Olga was a shot-putter for the Soviet Union. It was the height of the cold war, and all the world was aghast, not just because they crossed the lines between East and West, but because many people thought Olga was not quite lovely enough to inspire international romance. She defected for Harold and the two live happily together to this day.

The truth is that while male athletes love a good figure as much as the next man, their standards are somewhat different—and more attainable—than a centerfold body. Athletes like women who are in shape, who maximize what they inherited genetically. In his book, *Arnold's Bodyshaping for Women,* Arnold Schwarzenegger speaks of meeting a woman who was "too fragile inside and out—for me." He quickly forgot her. Four years later he ran into her in a shoe store and found her incredibly changed. She'd been running and training with weights and he was knocked out by her improvement. "Lisa had become far more feminine than she had been before as this fragile, insecure creature. To me, femininity has always indicated strength, character, and confidence."

Arnold is not that different from other athletes. It's no wonder that he ignored dozens of starlets to fall in love with the dynamic Maria Shriver.

"So you say I've got to spend four years getting in shape before I try to meet one of these men?" asks Susan, a softly rounded copy editor. "Forget it, I'll go back to the intellectuals and Fettuccini Alfredo."

"No," I tell Susan, "I don't mean that you have to be in fantastic shape. You just have to be *interested* in getting in shape and willing to join these men in the physical activities that build a healthy body."

Start by running in the park. Stick with the pack; there *is* loneliness for the long distance runner. When you pass a man, run abreast for a minute, wink and dash ahead. Laugh when he catches up. This is real social exercise, and the increased blood flow raises the most passive girl's assertion quotient. To help you feel confident, flatter your body. If your body is loose or too thin, wear shorts over sturdy insulated tights or choose an attractive sweat suit. Don't run until you're exhausted. Just enjoy yourself and you'll keep it up longer. (Passive/Active)

One of the fastest ways to get in shape and get fantastic men to help you do it is by joining a real gym. Not a "spa" or a "figure salon" or even a "health club" full of ferns and juice bars, but a place with a name like Midcity Gym or World Gym. It won't be quite as pretty as Bette's Fitness Salon, but it will be full of men, working out on the serious equipment experts recommend. These gyms do admit female members, but you won't find many there. And not, as you think, because the men resent them. Women just have not found out about gyms yet. They will. Most of the men who frequent these gyms are really very friendly and happy to help a woman who wants to improve her body. One story immediately comes to mind.

I recently covered a women's body-building event. In the warm-up room where the women were preparing to go on stage, one attractive, thirtyish blonde stood talking quietly to a hugely muscled, handsome young man. I was told he was her husband, so I thought I'd interview them both. She told me that she'd been living in Texas a year before, when she'd become interested in weight training. Not knowing how to begin, she went to the local gym and quickly spotted a man who looked like he knew what he was doing. She asked him what she should do to improve her legs. He was flattered that she'd asked him, assuming correctly, that she admired his physique, and he began working with her at the gym, instructing, helping and talking to her. In a few months they had become inseparable and he asked her to marry him, not caring that she was a few years his senior. She'd become so much more beautiful than any eighteen-year-old, he said. Go to the gym and, while working out, catch the eye of an attentive man. Smile and say, "Could you help me?" Admire his muscles, if only with your eyes at first and tell him what part of your own body you'd like to improve. Most men will be more than enthusiastic to show you their secrets. As your body becomes sleeker, shapelier, they'll all take notice. The only thing you have to lose is your old insecure image. (Passive/Active)

Check the small sports notices in your local paper to find out when and where local nonprofessional teams play. Almost every town has merchant-supported baseball, football or hockey teams. When you know who they are, call the sports editor at the paper and find out where they practice. Don't go to an actual game. The players will be keyed up and all their friends and fans will be there watching. Visit a practice session when the players are relaxed. Walk right up and call out "Hey, touchdown!" or "Good hit!" If they start showing off harder, you know you're making an impact. After practice, walk on the field and congratulate the players, especially the one who smiled at you after each throw. Invite him for a cool-down beer. (Active)

Or take a camera along. If you're shy, it gives you that all-important reason to be there and a reason to approach the man you want after practice and say, "I think I got a good shot of you catching that high ball. Could I make you a print?" You've singled him out and made him feel special: now get his address and be sure and send him the photo. He'll be very, very charmed. (Passive)

Cameras and tape recorders can help a shy seducer in many ways. When you have these tools, you have a reason to approach a man and a ready subject of conversation. Tell him you're interested in why men play sandlot ball, or school lot basketball. Can you talk to him some more at another time? Don't lie and say you work for a paper, just tell him you're personally interested and he seems to express himself so well. You are interested, are you not? (Passive)

It's so easy to meet athletes in sporting goods stores.

Even the men who work there are athletic and most stores carry clothing for women now, so you have a reason to be there. You will be noticed, but it's just because these stores don't have many female customers. You'll find it easy to strike up a conversation about the many unusual and beautiful sporting items. Ask other customers what some of the new equipment is used for. Men really do love to talk to a woman who seems genuinely interested in a sport. You're refreshing. By asking relaxed easy questions you can find yourself walking out with one of these men in the most natural way. (Passive/Active)

Spectator sports are a good example of where not to meet men. The guys are psyched for the game, and their vision is narrowed to the field or arena, cutting out all interest in meeting women. The men are with their male friends, all in their best beer-hall-buddy form. If you try to impress them with your knowledge of the game, you're competing. If you ask them to explain it, you're a dumb girl interfering with their comradery. If you try to talk about anything else, you're really out in the cold. If you like to watch the games, go and cheer your head off with the fellows. If you want to meet them, wait for another day.

Don't be afraid to be demonstrative with an athlete. They're comfortable with their bodies and at ease with physical contact. They won't take every tap, poke and squeeze as a sexual come-on and generally like a woman who's not too shy to squeeze their arm to make a point. You can even offer a shoulder massage to a tired athlete without him taking it the wrong way. He can probably use the massage, and he'll remember your touch and the good, warm feeling you engendered.

Remember to take what he loves seriously. Maybe you secretly think football is rough and dirty and a big waste of a Sunday, but if you like football players, develop an interest in the game. Find aspects of the sport that do interest you. Talk personalities and cute rear ends if you don't know the plays. Dress in nice athletic knits to show off that newly firmed figure of yours. Stretch out your legs, pat him on the shoulder, and flash him your biggest, healthiest smile. He'll appreciate you far more than any hothouse princess.

DOCTORS, LAWYERS AND OTHER PROFESSIONALS

Is there a mother anywhere who wouldn't burst with pride to be able to tell her friends "This is my son-in-law the doctor/lawyer/engineer?" Doctors, lawyers and other professional men have long been considered excellent husband material. If your heart beats as fast as mom's at the thought of a walk into the sunset with one of these white knights, this section is for you.

Doctors, lawyers and other highly trained professionals represent all that is positive about a "settlin' down" man. They exude money and stability, along with social position, intelligence and devotion to human betterment. They appear to be masculine perfection personified, but just keep in mind that behind this façade are some hard truths that are worth examining.

Doctors and lawyers are overworked, overstressed men with less time for socializing than most of us. This is one of the things that makes meeting the single doctor or lawyer so hard. The other barrier is the small number of single professionals available. Medical and law schools are tough and expensive. Unless a student has a rich daddy to back him, he finds himself struggling to keep up the work, pay the bills and have time or money for any social life at all. Consequently students training for one of the professions marry young. If you're the kind of woman who enjoys working for the future, you just may love helping such a man. Be warned though. If you're not a pretty sturdy woman, putting a man through college is a hard, unrewarding job. That's why so many of these men are divorced by the time they are established.

These divorced men socialize a little more than the students, but they're a lot more leery of involvement. A strong woman is what they need, but they may gravitate toward showy women instead, as a reward for all their hard work. If you remember to psych up and radiate strength while presenting yourself in your best clothes and makeup, you can appeal to them on both levels, and you may be the woman who walks off with the big prize.

Now let's find them.

I know a woman who always wanted to date a lawyer. A tireless *Ironside* fan, she was ready to commit a crime just to retain counsel.

"I imagine him visiting me in my cell," she once revealed, "telling me we'll win this case if it takes fifty appeals. And I say, 'Why do you work so hard for me?' and he takes me in his arms and says, 'Because I love you more than law itself.'"

One day a new woman came to work in her office who, wonder of wonders, was married to a young man in his second year of legal practice. My friend became close to her and discovered they had many things in common besides an interest in swooning in the arms of lawyers. She met her friend's husband, got along well with him as she did with her and at lunch a few days later she asked her friend outright, "Doesn't your husband have any single friends in his firm?" The next week it turned out the husband did have a single friend, who, at his wife's urging, was invited for dinner, along with another couple and the woman who loved lawyers. My friend charmed the briefs off the single lawyer and asked him for dinner at her place the following Tuesday. They've been together ever since.

Men do have single friends in their professions, and if you have a friend who dates, lives with or is married to a doctor, lawyer or other professional, let her know that you'd love to meet his friends. If you're a friend of his wife, a man is apt to describe you nicely to his colleague, laying all the groundwork for a successful pick-up. (Passive)

Before I became a writer and editor, I was a respiratory therapist working in hospitals. As a therapist I learned that some women really do go to nursing school because they love doctors. I also learned that very few doctors will date the nurses they work with in the hospital because they fear the gossip. Oh, I heard now and then of a doctor falling for his office nurse, but all in all, becoming a nurse didn't seem like a good way to date doctors. Becoming a hospital secretary, receptionist, transcriptionist or coffee shop volunteer, however, offered much better possibilities. That's because in most of these jobs the women weren't surrounded by a lot of co-workers, so the doctors could relax and talk with them. Asking a doctor if he's having a tough day is always a good way to start a conversation, and suggesting a great place you go to relax, a club, bar or hot-tub salon turns his attention to more personal thoughts. Tell him you know he misses out on a lot of fun and that it's a medical fact that we all function better if we balance work with pleasure. Make him laugh and let down his guard and he'll be ready to take you up on your suggestion. (Passive)

Check out a gym or handball court near the city courthouse. Lawyers need to unwind just as much as doctors do and are likely to choose a place near work to exercise between cases. Handball is an energetic sport, and if you learn to enjoy it, you'll meet many dynamic professionals. Not all will be lawyers, even if the court is across the street from the courthouse, but you can always check out his profession when you're mentioning a game of doubles.

In the gym, head for the Jacuzzi. It's always attractive to an overtaxed man facing a difficult afternoon. Say, "This feels so good when you're tense," and if he agrees, as he's sure to do, ask, "What do *you* do to get tense?" (Active)

If you like midnight snacks, try an all-night restaurant across the street from a hospital. Weary interns who escape there after the hospital coffee shop closes can be recognized by their white coats or "greens," a loose, green cotton pullover shirt. A sympathetic woman can say, "Is it worth it, doctor? All this suffering to save mankind?" It's the question he asks himself at such moments, opening him up to share his pains with you. For interns, one of the items high on their list of suffering is hospital cafeteria food. Suggest a good restaurant you know nearby. If he worries about the cost on his student stipend, say, "The world needs good doctors. I'd feel bad if you starved on my account. I'll split it with you." When any of us are weary, we appreciate a strong person coming along to give us support, and he's no exception. An assertive woman can go far with this approach. (Active)

The legal counterpart to the weary intern can be found in a nice bar near the courthouse around six in the evening. That nice looking but exhausted man can be approached with a cheerful, "Hard day, counselor?" If he's not a lawyer he'll tell you so, and you can say, "Sorry, I always assume everyone here is" to which he may very well point out the men who are, since most men in early evening bars are regulars and will know something about each other. Wish this first man a good evening and go say hello to whichever lawyer catches your eyes. (Passive/Active)

And if you really like lawyers, why not spend a day in court? Many of the lower courts, like civil court, traffic court or the courts that handle simple misdemeanors like shoplifting and prostitution are open to the public. Besides being a good place to see lawyers in action, court is an interesting experience.

If you spot a lawyer you like, follow him out after his case. Say, "I know it wasn't a big one, but I think you presented a really good case. If I ever need a lawyer, you're the man I want. Do you have a card?" And give him one of your cards so he remembers who cheered him with that flattery. (Active)

Students in professional schools—but especially law students—need to have a lot of typing done. If you can type, visit a local law, medical, architectural or engineering school and ask where the student bulletin board is. A message offering typing and transcription can bring you a lot of work, especially if you undercut the going rate by a few cents. A good idea is to offer to pick up and deliver. Once you're in his room, you can strike up a conversation, showing an interest in the material he gave you to type. Flatter his approach to the subject and ask about his studies. Ask, too, how the food is on campus. If he's as unimpressed as most students are with institutional cuisine, suggest a good restaurant or offer him a home-cooked meal if he'll bring his own typing over next time. (Passive)

A teaching hospital is a place where medical students go to do their time as interns and residents. Call to ask about the volunteer program, then request to put in your time on weekends. There are many more interns than doctors working weekends, and without the big guys around they're in a much livelier mood; just drop in to the coffee shop after your duties to see *how* lively. Saying "Are you a doctor?" is all the push they'll need to explain their importance in saving the world from disease and pestilence. (Passive/Active)

Those are a few ways to meet the elusive perfect catch. If you wondered why I didn't include going to doctors or lawyers with your problems, it's because a good man doesn't let himself get personally involved with a patient or client. And only the best will warm your dear old mother's heart.

ARTISTS, WRITERS AND MUSICIANS

There are many men you'll want to meet, but none presents a more romantic image than the artist. Eccentric, unpredictable, endlessly intriguing, these creative men have charmed queens and chambermaids alike through the centuries. George Bernard Shaw cynically explained, "The true artist will let his wife starve, his children go barefoot, his mother drudge for his living at seventy, sooner than work at anything but his art," and in a way that *is* part of the artist's great appeal. He is a man dedicated to his own ideals, instead of the dollar. And he can immortalize us. I don't think there's a woman who's ever desired an artist without dreaming of being his inspiration. There's nothing wrong with that dream, but to have it come true you must be perceptive. For one artist, inspiration is a wild, challenging, uncontrollable woman. Henry Miller felt this, once remarking, "I will sacrifice everything for the love of the unattainable, the elusive woman: money, wives, children, jobs, friendships, anything!"

Another man wants a strong, sensible woman who'll temper his own wildness. Another wants innocence. Another, intellect. There is an artist who can take inspiration from every woman and for every woman, an artist who will make a fascinating addition to her life.

If by artist you mean painter, sculptor or craftsman, rather than writer or musician, the first place to go is those much-mentioned gallery openings. Go straight for the food. All those people earnestly discussing the art are patrons, the artists have seen the work, and will be busy appreciating the wine and old friends. Approaching them with that knowledge isn't a bad idea. Listen in on a little conversation to see who is talking paints, chisels or clay and then say to the man you fancy, "You're one of the artists, right? I know you can always find them by the food." Laugh and hold his gaze so that he knows you're interested. (Passive/Active)

I know two friends who use a buddy system at openings. They split up at the door and spend a couple of hours circulating and talking, checking every once in a while to see what the other is up to. As the opening winds to a close, both women usually have found men they enjoy. When they drift back together one will say to the other, "I'm really hungry. Want to get something to eat?" Her friend agrees enthusiastically and they turn to their men, saying, "Come on. Let's all go." These good friends get by all the problems of going out with a girl friend by prior understanding and can get to know the men they've approached in a safe unpressured way. (Passive)

My friend Iris told me of a friend's bold approach to an art teacher. This friend had long admired his work, and when she saw that he was going to be teaching a course at a nearby college, she was eager to sign up. Then, going through the class description, she saw that he'd be including "life-studies drawing." Meaning he'd need a model. Rather than sign up for his class, she went directly to the man and asked if she could be his model in exchange for class time. He consented happily. She posed for three days and at the end of the third, she told him of a show at a nearby museum and asked if he'd like to see it. He said yes and asked her to dinner as well. Late that evening, over a bottle of wine, he admitted that he'd wanted to ask her out after her first day of modeling, because she'd projected an emotion in her posing that he felt was aimed at him.

Call the art departments of your local colleges. There will always be classes that need models, often nude, occasionally clothed. Don't worry about your body: art requires neither fashion model nor centerfold. In fact, a well-fleshed figure is more desirable to some artists, being closer to classic proportions. It's unlikely that you'll end up dating the teacher, but with a room full of artists, all concentrating on you, you'll find yourself catching one man's eye, smiling at him, and winding up in conversation after class. You can always work on homework together. (Active)

Helen is an average-looking girl, twenty-seven, who toys with a pottery hobby. She also loves artists and swears that the best way to meet them is through the magazines. *Craft Horizons, American Craft, Artform, Art News* and *Fine Woodworking* all tell where artists will be having shows and where they'll be teaching workshops. Helen zeroes in on the workshops.

She goes to class dressed to the teeth: extra make-up; loose, bouncy hair; tight jeans; and bright, thin provocative sweaters. Though she's not exactly a movie star, she stands out because most artists wear no makeup and utilitarian clothing. She's bright, friendly and inquisitive on top of making a notice-able appearance, and after class she's the one who takes the visiting artist to the local watering hole. Check the magazines and don't make the mistake of thinking you must look Bohemian to interest these men. A man alone in a strange town is ready for a little more excitement than that. (Passive/Active)

Writers are harder to find than painters and crafts-men. In large measure that's due to the solitary na-ture of their art, which can't be displayed in galleries or at parties. It can be taught in workshops, how-ever, just like any other art, and workshops are one of your best bets for meeting aspiring writers. Read your college brochures to find these evening and weekend courses and look particularly for the classes that feature well-known writers as guest lecturers. These will attract the largest numbers of interesting, serious writers, and that well-known guest could be the famous author or journalist you've always wanted to know. With fellow students, you can compare problems and writing styles, an integral part of the workshop teaching approach, leading to easy post-class pick ups. With that famous lecturer, consider your Famous Men approaches. He'll be mobbed after class, but if you can get to him before he speaks, tell him how much you admire his work and ask for the honor of buying him a drink later, there's a good chance he'll be flattered enough to join you for that cooling out in the local pub. (Passive)

And on the subject of pubs, writers may be the only artists who stake out one for their own in every major city. To find your city's writers' hangout, check the bars around the newspaper building. You'll always find one that bristles with journalists, and they're the easiest men you'll ever try to meet after they've spent a hard day at the keys. A lady I interviewed loves to talk current news with journalists because she's nosey and because they love to expound on their inside information. Ask what the real story is on something just starting to break in the papers and you've got a pick-up on the way to accomplished. (Active)

Remember the introduction to this section where I mentioned that men must buy the tools for their trade? Visit art supply stores or shops that sell musical instruments or sheet music. If you're interested in writers this is more of a problem, but you may discover a local stationery store that they patronize. Look at the racks of colored pencils, the little bottles of gilt paint, the silky, expensive brushes, the new guitars, even the best correction tape for a typewriter. Soon you'll notice curious men, rummaging along beside you. If they're eyeing the tools you're examining, it's because they're wondering what *your* specialty is. Smile at the man you like. Hold up the weird object you've just come upon, knit your brows, shrug your shoulders and say, "Do *you* know what it's for?" If he does, let him explain. If he doesn't, pull out another one and laugh together while you speculate on possible uses. This is a good time to ask what he does do, since you've learned what tools are outside his trade. He may act shy. Many artists are introverts and uncomfortable making claims about their work, so don't assume he's uninterested if he doesn't talk and joke immediately. If he continues to stick around, encourage him to tell you about the artists, writers or musicians who inspire his work. Ask who he likes. That may be easier for him to discuss than his own work. (Active)

If an artist you'd like to meet has a shop or showroom of his own, go in and court him while he works. Hopefully he'll have something small and inexpensive that you can afford. That's your initial reason for visiting. First tell him that you love his work but can't afford anything. Then, as you talk, convince yourself, out loud, that you must have something and take the small piece. The turnabout makes a much greater impression than your coming in and buying right away. In effect, you bought not only because you liked the work but because you came to like him.

Come back to his shop and tell him how much you enjoy what you bought. Tell him that soon you may be able to get something bigger. Every time you come in he'll say, "Come for your mural?" And you can reply, "No, the ship's coming in *next* week," leading to the day you feel bold enough to say, "I don't think I'll ever have the two thousand dollars, but I've got five dollars and twenty cents right now and I know a great place for cheap hamburgers." What starving artist can pass up a feast with admiring company? (Passive)

Musicians can be found in clubs, music stores and occasionally on street corners. A street-corner performer, and many of the best started this way, can be picked up by simply hanging around, complimenting him with some coins in his case, cup or hat, and offering a meal when he starts to pack up. He's in the street because he's not working and wants recognition. A musician visiting the club to listen to a band or performer who inspires him is a lot easier, if you can recognize him. Look for his devotional attention and simply ask, "Are you a musician, too?" It's flattering if he is or isn't and a comfortable way to find a man to enjoy the music with you. (Passive/Active)

Really successful musicians, usually defined as those who don't work at second jobs, have more in common with Famous Men than other artists. I suggest you refer to that section if your dreams are of Rod Stewart, Willy Nelson or Luciano Pavarotti.

When you've met that artist or craftsman, have visited his shop, seen his show and still can't think of a way to get his attention, think of a gift of found objects. A beautiful shard of glass, a twisted old light fixture, a doll's leg, or a bundle of dowels glimpsed in the trash might be just what an artist would love. Knowing his work is the key. Bringing a dead Christmas tree to a jeweler will get you in his nut file faster than in his black book. But when your find shows insight, like giving that bit of fine old glass to the stained-glass artist, you touch his heart. It's not quite a gift, so he's not uncomfortable, yet you've shown more thought for him than the average gift ever could. You're thinking not only of him, you're thinking of his art, the deepest flattery to that man George Bernard Shaw wrote of. And for all their oddities and shortcomings, creative men *are* the men most appreciative of romantic gestures. Maybe that's the real reason we love them.

CONCLUSION

Don't be afraid to look for your artist, writer or musician. Or for your rich man, your famous man, your doctor or lawyer. You *can* meet and pick up any of them. It's fun to meet and date the men we've fantasized about, but I'm sure that as you get out there and start picking men who appeal to you, you'll find that many a shoe salesman, computer programmer or accountant is as wonderful to be with as any of these "ideal types." The most important reason for this chapter is to help you understand that all these men are human. Learning that they all become sad, get sick, feel lonely, fall in and out of love, eat, do their laundry, take their dog to the vet at ten o'clock at night and even have moments when they wonder where they're going to meet the right woman, helps you realize that you are as special as they are. It can also make you realize that the man who really cares about you can be the most special man of all.

13

Special Moments

A long relationship has just ended. It was painful, those last couple of months. It hurt to decide finally it was over, but you're relieved too. The strain is easing, you two are learning how to be just friends, and you're starting to be able to think of new men and new relationships. For the first time since the breakup you're in a high, party mood. You want to go out and paint the town and proclaim your freedom, but it's just too soon for a new boyfriend. You sort carefully through your feelings and realize what you really want is a sexy, exciting man to hold you and touch you and whisper how great you are, boosting your injured ego and getting you back into the social whirl.

You're in a special mood and you're looking for a special kind of pick-up.

There was a time, in the very recent past, when no woman would admit to wanting instant intimacy. A trip to any singles bar on any Saturday night will show you how this has changed. Oh, there'll be many women just there to start a conversation, but there'll be others openly looking for immediate gratification.

We still want dates and boyfriends and lovers and husbands, but there are times, we now admit, when what we want most is a mad, passionate fling. I call these Special Moments.

A Special Moment can arise when you've just ended a relationship and want a man but aren't ready for a *new* relationship.

A Special Moment can be experiencing a fantasy man you're not suited to live with or date.

A Special Moment can be sparked when you look across the dance floor and see a man so breathtaking *you just can't wait.*

A Special Moment is the first thing that comes to your mind when you hear the words "pick up," and it can be done as easily and safely as any other pick-up you've learned about in this book.

Easier, since its the ultimate male fantasy.

When I mentioned singles bars you'll remember I said men go to them with the thought of having sex. They really go there with the *hope* of having sex, a hope very akin to fantasy for most of them. They don't quite expect it to happen. That's because most women still go to singles bars looking for relationships. The men's hopes and the women's counterhopes make for that undercurrent of tension.

When you save singles bars for your Special Moments, you strike a happy truce. Since you walk in wanting what the men want, the bar becomes a great big candy store. Go for the very best man you see. Special Moments are all about living your wildest dreams, and if this night is to be remembered with no regrets, don't "settle for," don't "accept." Pick up the sexiest, handsomest man in the place. Decide what you want and who you want and "accept" or "settle for" no substitutes.

The choice is all yours, and the following are some precise do's and don'ts that keep it that way.

1. Dress carefully. You want to attract but never look trashy. Think about the place you're going to and how the other women dress. The aim is to wear clothes that will make you more noticeable than at least half the other women. If dresses are the accepted look, wear a good quality one, cut lower in front, back or up the leg than you would usually dare. If it's jeans and western shirts, go for the beaded and feathered buckskin halter, knowing there'll be a few woman who'll outdo you with see-through or sequins. If your clothes are the flashiest, it looks like you're trying too hard, and you'll raise the competitive hackles of every other woman. If you're one of twenty top contenders, you'll get just the right kind of notice.

2. Go out when your mood is high. A fling is not a cure for depression. If you're looking for love and understanding, it's better to stay home and cuddle your dog and wait for a night when you feel more positive about yourself.

3. Select one or a very few men who appeal to you and concentrate your attention on him or them. Your mood may be wild, but flirting wildly with every man in the bar makes you seem cheap and indiscriminate. Its exciting to a man, even a very good looking man whom you'd never be comfortable approaching otherwise, to feel that he was chosen over all others. *Tell* him he was and show him he was by giving him all your attention.

4. Get close to the man who interests you, watch him and listen to him before you approach. You'll have less time to find out about this pick-up than any other man you'll meet, so get as many clues to his personality as you can before you speak. If he's acting too macho, too aggressive, if he's making disparaging or hostile remarks, pass him by. If he's just a normal guy, perhaps acting a little shy, try to open with a remark that will make you stand out in the sea of faces.

5. There's no time you'll need your humor and enthusiasm more than in a singles bar. You're tense, he's tense, the whole bar is tense, even though it's roaring with laughter and loud voices. If you say hello to him with a laugh in your voice and a blinding smile, he'll begin to relax. Laugh at the other patrons (kindly), laugh at his jokes, laugh at your own jokes and he'll think he's met a pretty great woman.

6. Don't drink too much to bolster your nerve. If you're going to leave a bar with a man, you want to

be in condition to do it under your own power and know where you're going. If you do get loaded or if he does, the only safe decision for you is to go home —alone.

7. If the man you're approaching is unusually attractive, look for something out of the ordinary to compliment. He knows his face is handsome, he knows his body looks like Bruce Jenner's, but perhaps he's never been told that he has the hands of a sculptor and that those broad palms make him look as strong as he is handsome. Tell him the combination is rare and much more attractive than mere beauty. You need a unique approach to catch the attention of a man who is used to being picked up.

8. This is a time for provocative body language. Touch his arm lightly for emphasis when you talk. Touch his shoulder or even his hip, but don't grab, and don't hang on him. Your light, stroking touch and sinuous movements on the dance floor are a tease, a message to him that you're a woman in touch with her body and comfortable with a man's. Definitely compelling.

9. When you know you've connected with the man you want, get him out of the bar—to another public spot. A restaurant or coffee shop is the perfect halfway stop between home or hotel. You can both wind down a little and make sure you want to proceed. Saying to him in the bar, "Let's get away from all these people," will have him moving for the

door and as you hit the street you can suggest that hamburger at the restaurant on the corner.

10. Go to his home or a hotel. Most women feel more secure in their own homes, but, without dwelling on the slim chance of trouble, it's easier to leave his house when he doesn't want you to go than it is to get a man who outweighs you by sixty pounds out of *your* house if he decides he doesn't want to leave. And wouldn't you rather watch out for his valuables than worry about your own? A hotel can be ideal. Besides being romantic, a hotel fling means the desk knows where you are and nobody has to worry about knocking over the other's priceless heirloom bedlamp.

11. If you're a shy woman who can't imagine going to a singles bar and doing any of this, but you wish you could, try a hotel bar. It will be much quieter and less competitive and the men will always outnumber the women. You'll find fewer hunks, but if three-piece-suit men appeal, you'll have a good time. You can start a conversation just by saying "Hi" to these lonely traveling men, and since they're staying at the hotel "where to go" is never a problem.

12. Make birth control your responsibility. This is your moment, your fling, so come prepared. Never let yourself go unprotected into unknown territory.

Now for some cautions. Don't be alarmed, be forewarned and safe. Every adventure has possible dangers but you can be safe with the man you've picked up if you look out for the signs of trouble.

1. Don't go anywhere you can't leave under your own power. If a man lives far out in the country, take separate cars or suggest splitting the bill for a room in town.

2. Don't go anywhere with more than one man unless you feel very sure of the situation. If the friend is nice and nonaggressive and the man you're with shows respect and has a clear understanding that you're with him because you like him very much and not just because he was the first to look at you, the friend or roommate needn't be a problem. However, if they're talking "party," you may have more on your hands than you can handle. The same goes for getting to a man's house and finding several friends inside when he opens the door. That may be the time to say, "I just remembered I left the water running," and run yourself, before even going in.

3. Respect him and his property. Perhaps you expect never to see him again, that's still no reason to laugh at him, be mean to him, drop your ashes on the carpet, spill your drink on his coffee table or leave his towels in the bathtub. Treat every man as someone you'd want for a life-long friend and he'll treat you with the respect that'll keep it a happy experience.

4. Don't start games you can't stop. Special Moments are a time to play out fantasies, but if your fantasies run to ropes or mock rape, save them for a

man you know well. Never let a man you don't really know tie you up, blindfold you or put a gag in your mouth.

5. Don't criticize him if he doesn't live up to your fantasy. You may not have lived up to his. When two people come together in something as complex as sex, no one can guarantee the outcome. If it doesn't work out, just tell him you're glad to have met him and leave gracefully, happy that the incompatibility wasn't in a relationship where it could be a real problem.

6. Don't give him your phone number if you really don't want to see him again. Letting him call you and telling him over and over that you're busy is no way to spare his feelings. Say before you go home that you enjoyed your time with him, that he's a nice person, that tonight was an adventure you'll remember warmly, but that it's an adventure that can't be repeated. When he wants to know why, say you can't really explain, that's just how it has to be. If you draw rejection out past this night, it will become painful for both of you.

7. On the other hand, if you want to see him again, don't feel your Special Moment has to remain a fling. If you've followed the advice here, he's feeling good about you and will have no doubts about your "niceness." Ask if he'd like to get together again, with no apologies.

8. Don't pick up any man unless it's really what you want to do. Being "talked into it" doesn't count,

figuring you "have nothing to lose" doesn't either, and I don't want to hear about "it was the only way I could keep him," better known in my day as "proving your love."

Choosing to go to bed with a man also means choosing who you won't go to bed with. Seeing a man who excites you, discovering that he can share your excitement and arranging to act out your desires can be a liberating, thrilling Special Moment. "Giving in" is just old-fashioned submission.

14

From Pick-Up to Partner

There will come a time when you realize a man you've picked up is really special, someone you'd like to see again and again, and maybe the person you want to live with or even marry. You're thrilled, excited and a little sick in the pit of your stomach. It feels so good and it's so scary because, even though you could pick him up, you're not sure how to keep him. There must be a way to act that will make the man with whom you share so many interests fall lastingly in love with you. How do you jump from the carefree girl who picked him up to the woman he'll take seriously? How do you interest him enough that he'll want to stop shopping around?

Humans are the most inquisitive animals on this planet. Take the lion. He is content to eat, sleep and hunt the same territory every day. He has no need for new challenges. He never gets the urge to cross the jungle, risking his life just to see if there's better hunting on the other side. Even chimps, incredibly curious animals, will not risk their lives or mates for new experiences.

Humans are different. We constantly compare what we have to what our neighbor has, and we need fresh mental and physical stimuli not only to grow, but simply to maintain our feelings of well-being. Now if you're wondering what Anthropology 101 has to do with making that man you've picked up love you, let's consider why he was so responsive to your picking him up in the first place. When you walked up and started a conversation, letting him know that you liked the way he looked and that you wanted to get to know him better, you showed yourself as an assertive, exciting woman. A woman with enthusiasm for life. That not only gave him immediate mental and physical stimulation, it promised stimuli to come. It is later, when the relationship is established, that a lot of women make their fatal mistake. Once the man starts pursuing them, they settle back into passivity.

He wants the excitement to go on. He wants to feel the electricity when you're together and he wants to feel that everywhere you go, everything you do, is a fresh new adventure. He wants to feel that he's the most important man in your life and he wants to know that it's *him* you want, not his compliments or "I love yous" or a warm body beside you. Set the tone of your relationship at your first meeting.

Approach every pick-up as a potential steady.

When you meet a new man, treat him as an individual. Don't make him feel that he's one of a string of pick-ups by talking about other boyfriends or taking him to a bar where all the men wink and wave at you. That may boost your ego, but he'll resent your lack of consideration for his comfort and possibly begin to resent you. Instead, concentrate on him. Meet his eyes and listen to what he says. Sometimes we're so concerned with making our own impact that we use the time while he's talking to formulate our next witty comment. This inhibits any real communication. He'd much rather hear a well-considered response on his subject than a stand-up comedy routine—if he's hoping to go further with you.

If you hope to go further, think before bringing him home. Framed photos of old boyfriends are trophies he doesn't need to face. Letters and loving notes left out on a dresser or kitchen counter may spur some men to competition, but others will see them as obstacles, encouraging them to write you off as a serious relationship. Men's clothing on the bathroom hook, even if it's that old shirt you sleep in, and extra toothbrushes make some men feel more like numbers than names. And if your books are inscribed "To Rhonda from Kissy Lips," leave them in the bookcase instead of on the coffee table.

First impressions are very important, and if his first trip to your home says there's a line ahead of him, he may go for the quick checkout.

Calling a man early in a relationship when you

just want to talk is hard to do, but if you call him because you've just heard something that he'd love to know about, a joke on a favorite subject, or a piece of news relating to one of his heroes, he will feel you two are really on the same beam, encouraging him to think of you when he has some news he wants to enjoy with someone. You've shown enthusiasm for his life, so you don't even have to share his interest in the subject for the phone call to make you closer. He's happy that you're thinking of *him*, not your *relationship* to him.

Show him you have a sense of adventure. Suggest a night at the local mud wrestling bar, at an erotic movie or at a real honest-to-goodness burlesque house, if your town has one. These are places he'd love to explore but may feel he could only attend with his male buddies. It's all pretty harmless fun, but if he goes with the guys, you're apt to sit at home grumbling and feeling left out. If you suggest this night out, and you can cite curiosity as your motive, you'll know exactly what goes on, and he'll be thrilled to find a woman open enough to explore life's more daring experiences with him. The plus here is that he's more likely to be honest with you in the future, confiding his fantasies instead of seeking to fulfill them elsewhere.

Caring about each other more than petty victories is the essence of positive loving. Don't make the mistake of thinking it weak to compromise your own interests occasionally to maintain the happiness of your relationship. Equality is not measured by a single act. Sometimes you'll go with him to a company picnic and talk with the boss you despise so that next week he'll go to Ocean World with you, even though he hates fish. It's easy to keep up your enthusiasm when you're both doing what you like, but the relationship that grows is the one in which you are willing to find something to enjoy in a place that you must attend for the other's sake. If you do it for him, he's likely to do it for you, giving you equality *and* the flexibility necessary for a really lasting relationship.

Sometimes a little compromising right up front can help save you from unpleasant compromises later. Perhaps he wants to take you for a week-long camping trip. You've never roughed it more than sleeping the night on a lumpy couch and you're ready to decline outright. Reconsider. Don't commit yourself for the week in the Rockies, but tell him you'll be happy to try an overnighter in the nearby national forest. Once you're there, you may decide that one night on the ground is enough for that year, but knowing it's just one night makes it a lot easier to smile about the experience. Later, when you're back home, you can tell him camping isn't really for you. He'll appreciate your good-natured effort, and it will now be easier for you to strike a happy compromise for future trips. Something like renting a camper or staying three nights in motels to two nights on the ground. It's more important that you accept and support his interests than share them all.

And while we're considering compromise, remember that every time together can't be a night on the town. Formal dates are extravagant fun, but as long as you're spending all your time in planned activities, he'll be thinking of you as a date. When you want him to start considering you as someone to love and live with, you'll have to show him you can inject enthusiasm into ordinary daily life.

It doesn't take a lot of effort to make an evening at home enjoyable. Ordinary food can be a great meal if you serve it with imagination. Spread a tablecloth on the living room floor, turn on some music, light some candles, break out wine or beer and a rich gluttonous dessert and have a city picnic. Use paper plates so there's no clean-up rush. He'll be more satisfied than he would be in a stuffy restaurant where he has to pay and get home before he can cuddle you.

I remember a great dinner eaten with a friend ten years ago. He showed up in cut-offs on a hot summer day with three pounds of crab legs and a pint bottle of mayonnaise. I put on a bathing suit, spread some newspapers on the front porch and we fell to cracking the crabs, dipping them in the mayonnaise and passing some jug wine I had in the refrigerator. We just dropped the shells on the papers while we laughed and talked. It wasn't a romantic meal by any definition, but it was fun, spontaneous and deliciously abandoned. Even a night watching TV can be satisfying if you use your imagination. Make some popcorn together, adjust the lighting to a warm, romantic glow and snuggle under a quilt on the couch with some interesting magazines to share during commercials.

The point is that anything you do with him can be more exciting than what he does with someone else *if* you bring enthusiasm and good humor to the situation. When you can make staying home more fun than going out, you're almost there. The only area left to work on is your special, private time, the time for physical enthusiasm, when you take your new love into the bedroom.

In talking to all the men and women I've encountered while writing this book, I've asked those who've been involved in serious relationships, "How important was the quality of the sex with your partner in establishing your love for him or her?" Here are some answers.

Ellen, age twenty-eight: "Every relationship that ever had significance for me started with a strong sexual rapport."

Rick, age thirty-one: "After establishing interests in common, it's a great sexual relationship, one where we understand each other's needs, that makes me fall in love."

Peter, age twenty-two: "It didn't make me love her, that she was so tuned in to me in bed. It just tied all the other things I loved about her together and made me know I didn't want to go through any night without her."

Allen, age forty: "For me it's the time after the sex. When we lie there holding each other, it's the closest I can be to another human. It's that feeling that makes all the little stuff we don't agree on meaningless."

Tish, age thirty-three: "Making love to a man I love is the best thing in the world, heaven on earth. Making love to a man I like a whole lot can make me start thinking of calling it love, if the fireworks are there."

The conclusions were fairly consistent. Making love to a man who has no strong feelings for you will not make him love you. Making wonderful, joyous love with a man who already likes you quite a bit *can* be a big factor in deepening his feelings to real love.

Knowing how to make love to a man in the way that will touch his deepest emotions is not hard. It doesn't require any complicated acrobatics. It only requires your enthusiastic commitment to your man, the moment and your own satisfaction. Let's start with your man.

A man loves to know that his woman is totally involved with him during sex. A woman who is totally aware of the man she's with sees, feels and hears her cues in making love to him. When she brushes his thigh with the tips of her nails she feels the shiver of pleasure ripple his skin. When she switches to a fimer, flat-palmed stroking and feels his muscles relax she realizes that he prefers the light tickling touch. If his body cues aren't strong enough for her to interpret in the beginning, the aware woman will say, "Does this feel good? Does this?" instead of the helpless, unenthusiastic "What do you want me to do?"

A fine way to develop your awareness and increase your involvement is to map his erogenous zones. Sound difficult, clinical? It's neither and really a wonderful prelude to any act of love.

First, consider all the places on his body where he's most likely to enjoy stimulation. They are: the ears, the sides of his neck down to the ridge of his collarbones, the hollow of his throat, his armpits, nipples, navel, the lines of sensitivity traced from hipbone to groin, the cleft of his buttocks and anus, the inner thighs, backs of the knees and his feet. You know, of course, about the penis and scrotum.

Now think of all these potential erogenous zones as forming a path down his body. Place your fingertips gently on his face and trace downward slowly from his temples. Tickle and trace the rims of his ears, dipping behind them to pick out the prominent muscle that leads down his neck into his collarbones. Let your fingers gently explore the hollows above the bones, following them into the hollow of his throat. Sweep down into his armpits, trace up the soft undersides of his arms and tease the hairs gently with your fingertips. Move up to his nipples, advancing with loose circular swirls. Brush the areola, the dark area around his nipple, with that sime circular motion, interspersed with lightly rolling his nipples between thumb and forefinger. Your man may be moaning by now but don't linger too long. File that spot as one to remember and trace down to his navel, tickling the edge and moving on to the exquisitely ticklish line from hipbone straight into his groin. Don't stimulate his penis just yet. Instead, ruffle his pubic hair, and move down between his slightly spread legs to tease the tips of the hairs on his buttocks and the crease that hides his anus. Move very slowly in this area; the sensitivity changes from inch to inch, and you can get a feel for the exact spots that trigger intense pleasure by going slowly. Now stroke the thighs just below his groin. Tickle the hairs and spider-step down to the sides and backs of his knees, a surprisingly sensitive zone. And when you slide down his calves to massage, tickle and gently pull on his toes, you've completed your journey.

To take this journey on your special man you'll want to kneel beside him on the bed or sit astride for the most comfort. You may also wish to use your lips, tongue and teeth to help your fingers find the path to his individual arousal points. Always start gently, when you find him sighing and his muscles tightening at some of the stops, say softly, "Is that nice? Would you like more pressure?" Even if he has trouble expressing himself, his physical response will let you know what he enjoys. And let him know that his body is exciting you.

When you look at his body and your breath quickens, it excites a man immeasurably. When you can't wait for him to undress you, but begin taking your clothes off for him, he can hardly wait to make love to you. When you run your hands sensuously over your own body, lingering on your own erogenous zones (breasts, abdomen, thighs), you stir a man's natural voyeuristic interest to a tempest. And when you simply say, "You make me so hot," you make him impatient to take you to bed.

Just as it's a myth that men always want to be the aggressors in picking up a woman, it's a myth that most want compliant women who force them to make all the moves in seduction. Anything you do that shows your man that you are aroused *by him* and want to make love to him for the pleasure it will bring you will make him think he's found a pretty great lover. Your man really doesn't want to use your body; he wants to use *his* body with you using *your* body so that you both achieve the satisfaction you desire.

Going even further, many men dream of women *taking* pleasure from their bodies, asking for or taking their hands or penises and guiding them in the way that gives the greatest satisfaction. Just as you deserve all the other human rights, you deserve sexual pleasure. You need never feel guilty about experiencing arousal and you will make your man love you more when you ask warmly, passionately for the pleasure he can give you.

Remember, making love is the expression of your strongest affections and it should only arise out of those moments when you feel the closest. When you are angry about something or insecure, your sex will be clinging and self-conscious. You will be trying to prove that you love him instead of feeling free to simply enjoy yourself. Many lovers end a fight by going to bed. It can be very active, passionate sex, but often it's not making love, as your feelings afterward will tell you.

In the early days of your relationship, when you want your sex to deepen your feelings for each other, think of it as frosting on the cake. When you've just spent an evening looking into each other's eyes, really exchanging ideas and laughing together over the little things you both enjoy, *that* is the time to take your feelings into the bedroom, when you will expand and solidify them by making the most exhilarating love possible.

So as you see, making a pick-up something more is not so difficult. You must share interests and you must share a certain physical attraction, but beyond those factors, you need only an open, enthusiastic view of life. We're all drawn to happy people. If that happy energetic person is you, the man you want to see more of will want to see more of you.

15

Taking Action

Convinced that men really want to be picked up?
Comfortable that you, whatever your personality,
can pick up a man without hurting his ego, looking
cheap, getting a Goodbar or giving your mother a
coronary? You should be. Men are as human and
as hungry for friendship as any of us. Of all the
people I talked to, men were the most supportive
of my writing this book because they all wanted to
see more women freely pursuing their desires. Every
man I spoke to said he'd be thrilled to be approached
by women, if he hadn't been already, and the men
who had been lucky enough to meet women unafraid to make the first move all mentioned it as a
memorable experience, even when it led to nothing
more than a drink and a few minutes of conversation.

Getting picked up in the right way makes a man
feel masculine and attractive. It makes him feel
good and it makes the woman picking him up look

better than the helpless women who sit and wait. The right way to pick up a man is what this book is all about, and put together properly the easy steps I've described really do work. They'll calm you, calm him, create the attitude you want to project, lead the conversation where you want it to go and help you to an outcome you'll both enjoy. You'll never know how much life you're missing until you go out and look for it, but if you're still a little nervous, read my five success stories. They were all told to me by friends or women I encountered in my research. All are true and none would have happened if the women hadn't dared to take the first step.

KEKO, WHO WAS TOO SHY

Keko was shy, but shyness was only half the barrier that kept her from meeting men. She came to America with her widowed mother and grandmother from a small village in Japan and her upbringing was very traditional. By the time she was twenty-four, her life had fallen into a lonely sameness; by day, she worked at calligraphy for a printing firm. In the evenings, while her mother and grandmother addressed envelopes for their living, she painted watercolors, incorporating the native trees around their Seattle, Washington, home into Japanese themes. She longed for a boyfriend, but her mother was suspicious of the ill-mannered American men and cautioned her to wait until a proper Japanese man could be found. Keko, at twenty-four, stopped believing he'd ever come along.

But he did. He came into the art director's office to discuss a new card design, and his attention was caught by the painting hanging over the paste-up table.

"Who did this watercolor?" asked Izumi. "I don't see any mark or signature."

"Our calligrapher," replied the art director. "She wouldn't even take money for it, let alone sign it. She's one of your 'Oh it is worthless' modest kind of Japanese girls. Really old-fashioned." They didn't know Keko could hear them in her cubicle, and she burned with embarrassment when the art director called her in to meet her admirer. Izumi was clearly an American Japanese; his suit was impeccably cut, but his hair was loose and casual, has face was open and bold like the American men her mother feared, but he was also so handsome his gaze made Keko feel very shy and agitated. Keko knew this was the man she'd waited for.

Izumi wanted a painting and he insisted on knowing her price. "They're not good enough," she said instinctively, and immediately remembered what she'd heard the art director say about modesty and burned with shame at her traditional response.

"I'll simply pay you what *I* know it's worth, then," Izumi said and slipped her a card with his address and office number, lettered, she saw, by her own pen.

She worked every night for two weeks to make a magnificent painting for Izumi. She imagined his face when she'd give it to him, pictured him falling in love with her when he saw how hard she'd worked, how inspired she'd been. She was sure if the painting was good enough he'd ask her to share dinner with him. She told her mother nothing, for fear she'd say, "Is he American?" and then forbid her to see him.

His office was much bigger and more modern than she'd ever imagined. Everywhere there were pretty American secretaries with bold stares and loud voices. And paintings. There were paintings on every wall, several on some. He *collects* them, she realized, and it came to her that bringing him one more, no matter how inspired, would never be enough to make him want her. Looking at the brash young secretaries, she knew it was going to take much more than a modest blush and artistic talent to have the man she wanted.

Izumi called Keko into his office and took the painting from her hands. "Beautiful, just beautiful," he said and was surprised to see she held her eyes steady on his. "Now I will give you some money no matter what you say," he continued and was even more surprised to hear coming from her mouth, albeit weakly, "Thank you, the price is fifty dollars. Izumi."

"Ho, and I heard you were one of those modest girls." How she blushed then, how she wanted to lower her eyes and take back her words. But Izumi looked pleased. He said, "It's worth every nickel. You're a great artist." Keko smiled and blushed so hard she thought she would faint, but still she said, "I worked extra hard so you would like it. Because I like you." Izumi smiled broadly, "Talented, pretty and flatterer, too. You know you're going to get to me if you don't watch out." And perhaps because that made her feel truly faint, Keko forgot all her mother's warnings and said the unsayable: "Would you like to share a lunch then, sometime?" "How about cocktails?" Izumi answered, "Right now?"

It would be untrue to say that Keko is no longer shy, but now at twenty-five, she lives in her own apartment, never fears that she'll not have a man and at night, when her work is done, she is almost never lonely.

RANDY AND THE LASTING RELATIONSHIP

The year she turned nineteen, Randy celebrated her freedom by spending the whole summer with her girl friend on an island off the New Jersey coast. By day they tanned, by night they hung out at the Acme Bar, and when that long summer of first freedoms crept toward September, Randy saw a new boy in the Acme who looked just like a boy she'd tried, unsuccessfully, to attract for three years. She vowed that this time she would be successful. The

Acme had a circular bar, and three nights in a row she sat across from him, waited to catch his eye, raised her glass and mouthed, "Want a beer?" For two nights he waved no, so on the third, when he repeated the gesture, Randy got up, walked over to him and asked, "Can we drink ours together then?"

He was happy to do that, explaining he'd just been embarrassed to ask her to buy him one. His name was Christopher, and they talked until Randy's friend persuaded her, reluctantly, to go home.

It was three nights before Christopher returned to the bar. Then he was back, celebrating his birthday with a huge group of friends and Randy happily joined in. They laughed together and talked and she planned to ask if they'd see each other when the summer ended, but before she could, his friends picked him up bodily and carried him out of the bar, off to a private party.

"I can't let it end this way," Randy suddenly realized. "I'm not going home on Saturday never to see him again." She ran out of the bar. Christopher's friends were carrying him up a hill, still laughing and hooting, blind to Randy as she raced up the opposite side of the street. When the group reached the crest of the hill, Randy was perched on a fence, breathing hard. Seeing her, the friends dropped Christopher, who picked himself up and asked, "What are you doing here?"

"I couldn't let you get away," she replied, shocked by her own honesty. Christopher was stunned. He'd never been pursued by a woman, and he quickly bid his friends good night and asked Randy to take a walk on the beach with him.

They walked all night and Christopher told Randy how exciting it was to find a woman so strong, so sure of herself. Randy had never planned to be that strong, but it felt good, and it felt even better that Christopher liked her strength and was holding her and making plans to return to the city with her.

Three years later, Randy is still feeling strong and loving Christopher who's happy to have found this pioneering woman who knew what she wanted and wasn't afraid to chase after it.

KATHY'S SPECIAL MOMENT

Like Randy, Kathy was spurred to pick up a man very much like one who got away. Unlike Randy, the man who left was a boyfriend, and Kathy's ego was devastated. She had fallen in love with a big, red-haired Irish soccer player at the college where she taught. As their relationship heated up, the young athlete got nervous. He'd initiated the affair, but when Kathy responded so ardently, he finally admitted he had a fiancée back home and had never intended to get so involved. When Kathy was unable to treat their affair casually, he transferred back to Dublin, leaving her heartbroken.

She thought of him every day and found herself whirling around whenever a red-haired man passed her on the street. Though lonely, she couldn't imagine looking up into any face that wasn't his. Then at a seminar, a month after he'd gone, she saw a face that could have been his double.

It belonged to a teaching fellow from another college. He was older than her soccer player, but also from Ireland, just as tall and just as red-haired. She introduced herself and asked how he was enjoying the seminar. They talked and after about half an hour, Kathy ventured, "Isn't it stuffy in here? Let's go get a cup of coffee and come back for the speakers."

Kathy had three cups of coffee and a peach cobbler while working up her nerve. The man was actually quite interesting, but it was his face, so much like her ex-boyfriend's, that fascinated her. Finally, he gripped her hand to make a point and she blurted out, "I hope you don't think I'm too forward, but I know a hotel near here and I don't care a thing about hearing those speakers." He waved for the waitress and kissed Kathy's hand.

The afternoon passed into a long evening of bliss. Where Kathy's intensity had frightened the immature soccer player, this older man revelled in what he called her inner fire, and he told her repeatedly that meeting her was like a fantasy fulfilled.

And Kathy? She felt renewed, exorcised of her demons. She still wasn't ready for another relationship, somewhat to her new friend's disappointment, but when the old boyfriend's face rose up to haunt her, she could now put this new one over it, caught in a moment of ecstasy, and arrest the pain.

Kathy's current boyfriend is dark and Italian, with strong emotions to match her own. He's a very nice guy, but I couldn't resist asking her what ever become of her Irish teacher. "We trade letters about three times a year," she told me. "We write about our jobs and who we're seeing and then we replay memories of those fabulous five hours and talk about what we'll do if the right moment ever comes around again."

SHELLEY AND THE FAMOUS ACTOR

Shelley loves the theater. One of the reasons she moved to New York City was to be near Broadway. She often joked that new plays were her only vice, and she fantasized about dating the men whose performances were most moving. It was a special day indeed when Eric walked into the store where she worked selling collectibles and antique toys. Shelley had seen Eric just a few weeks ago in the play that was making him famous, and when he came in, tall, curly haired and handsome, her heart jumped, her hands trembled and she found herself begging the manager, "Please let me wait on him."

He collected antique model trains and was quite impressed with Shelley's interest in his hobby. She never let on that she knew who he was, afraid that he'd see her as one more groupie. When he finally selected an engine and prepared to go, she knew she had to act fast, so gripping the showcase to still her quaking, she said, "I'd love to see your collection sometime. I'm off on Sundays and Mondays."

"Certainly," he replied, "I love to find another train lover." And set a time for the following Sunday.

Shelley did a fast brushup on toy trains and arrived at his airy duplex dressed to knock 'em dead. They talked about many things that afternoon, including his profession, and Shelley admitted she'd seen the show and loved his performance. As the afternoon progressed Shelley discovered she really liked Eric for himself. She began asking what kind of trains he was most eager to find, repeating their names to herself until they were securely filed in her memory. Once, when he was out of the room, she even copied down his phone number.

The next day Shelley called every dealer, auctioneer and secondhand store she'd ever dealt with. By afternoon she'd found what she was looking for and nervously dialed Eric's apartment.

"Hi," she said, "this is Shelley. I just heard there's going to be a huge toy auction on the twenty-first that'll have two of those American Flyers you're looking for. I'll be buying for the store; would you like me to bid for you?"

Eric was so surprised—and delighted—he didn't even ask how she'd gotten his number. All he cared about was going to the auction with Shelley.

Afterward Shelley took Eric and his new train to dinner. That dinner led to more dinners. And nightclubs and lunches and warm summer days at the beach. Shelley still works at the antiques-store, but now she has three loves: theater, toy trains and Eric.

ONE GREAT AFTERNOON

I was never a popular teenager. I was part of that misfit legion, whose noses and names are too long, whose clothes never fit and whose tongues never form clever enough comments to transcend the awkwardness. I even began to accept my lot until a simple little event in my fifteenth summer hinted at a wonderful world beyond junior high.

I had decided to spend the afternoon at the local amusement park, by myself, losing quarters in the arcade. I was shooting tanks when I noticed a boy plugging space ships two machines down. He was older, maybe seventeen, thin with large dark eyes and a flickering smile. Most important, he was also alone, and for some reason I began to fantasize about talking to him. Usually such thoughts frightened me, but he glanced over once and before I turned away I saw . . . sympathy? No, empathy. His look was wary, but he too was eager for conversation. When I next looked up, he was standing drinking a soda and looking at me.

At last I just couldn't hold out. Turning, I stammered, "Do you know where to get a soda?" He blushed from his grin to those big eyes and handed me his.

An hour later I was telling him things I'd never confided to anyone. We were so much alike that we even talked about our shyness without being shy. I told him I wanted to be a doctor and an artist and he didn't even laugh. He wanted to be an actor and showed me how to juggle three Snickers bars. We went on a ride I'd always been afraid of, and he held my hand, and we ate two cones of cotton candy as reward for living through it.

In short, I had the best day of my early adolescence, and yet when we realized we were both overdue for dinner, we made no move to exchange phone numbers, to set future dates. The day had been perfect and we were both content to leave it as one beautiful, unblemished memory. He'd helped me to see that I could have as many friends as I wanted, and perhaps I did the same for him. Most of all, I learned to appreciate moments that day. Dates are great, relationships are wonderful, but the good ones are all just collections of happy moments. If we're to fully appreciate any of our social contacts, we have to learn to enjoy a conversation, a dance, or a dinner for the immediate pleasure it gives, instead of thinking about the relationship it may lead to. If I'd never enjoyed that day in the amusement park, I might never have known how to be really happy with that fun-loving man I picked up and eventually married.

HOW TO PICK UP A MAN

The choice is all yours. Any man you pick up can become a date, a one-night fling, a long relationship or just a happy day in the park. There's no set outcome to any pick-up, unless you have one in mind. As a male friend told me, "Women have no idea how much power they have over men." He's so right. It's always been the woman who said yes or no and allowed a relationship to start. Now that you can pick up a man, you can not only say who you'll go out with but actually go up to the man you want, let him know you want him and have exactly the kind of relationship you're looking for. Your social power becomes almost limitless, and that improves your overall confidence. When you can approach a stranger with ease, you can also speak out in a business meeting, hail a cab or a waiter, complain to the dry cleaner without being intimidated and even tell a man you care for exactly how you feel without fear of rejection.

To make the most of our opportunities, we all need to know how to say what we feel and ask for what we want. When we ask, we stand a much greater chance of having, and the more often we have what we really want, the happier and stronger we feel. If *you're* ready for a happier, stronger, more self-aware you, picking up a man isn't such a bad place to start.

ABOUT THE AUTHOR

Dian Hanson, born in Seattle, Washington, went into journalism after a brief career as a respiratory therapist. As a journalist, she helped start three magazines and did occasional freelance writing. Now managing editor of *Oui* magazine, Dian lives in New York City with her photographer husband, Little Bobby Hanson, and her stepson.

SIGNET Books of Related Interest

Buy them at your local

bookstore or use coupon

on next page for ordering.

More Reading from SIGNET and MENTOR